LOOKING BACK AT BRITAIN

VICTORIANS
COME OF AGE

1850s

LOOKING BACK AT BRITAIN

VICTORIANS
COME OF AGE

1850s

Helen Varley

Reader's Digest | gettyimages

CONTENTS

1850s IMAGE GALLERY

COVER, FRONT: Brunel and colleagues looking concerned at the first attempted launch of the *Leviathan* (later the *Great Eastern*) on the Thames, in December 1857. It took till the end of January to get the ship afloat.

COVER, BACK: An elderly lady in her Bath chair, with her young companion, photographed in 1854.

TITLE PAGE: Captain Henry Duberly of the 8th Hussars with his wife Frances Isabella during the Crimean War, 1855.

OPPOSITE: Ladies' crinolines being loaded onto a London omnibus going from Sloane Street to Fleet Street in 1854.

FOLLOWING PAGES:

Young cricketers getting ready for a game at the end of the 1850s.

A man and woman chatting across a country lane and wattle fence in southwest England, 1857.

Housing and boats at low tide along the Thames riverside in Lambeth, London.

Two girls in bonnets and layered dresses playing on an improvised see-saw.

THE **GREAT** EXHIBITION

From June 1850, London's Hyde Park resounded to the noise of construction work as the building to house the Great Exhibition rose at break-neck speed. Crowds gathered to watch the building go up and to spot celebrities, in particular Queen Victoria and Prince Albert, who visited frequently to review progress. The exhibition opened the following May and was a runaway success, due in no small part to its stunning stage – the Crystal Palace.

SURVEYING PROGRESS The open colonnade and garden front of the Crystal Palace, under reconstruction in Sydenham, South London.

A GRAND STATEMENT

The impact of the Great Exhibition reverberated through 19th-century Britain, promoting an awareness of the nation's achievements and a new sense of national identity. The idea of an exhibition of national industry was nothing new. The 1840s had seen exhibition fever in Europe – Bern, Madrid, Brussels, Bordeaux, St Petersburg and Lisbon had all staged events, and Paris had held no fewer than 11 Expositions since 1798. But London's Great Exhibition of 1851 would outshine them all. Staged in a fairy-tale iron-and-glass palace, it was by far the biggest event of its kind, but what made it truly groundbreaking was that the exhibitors came not just from Britain but from all over the world. The 'Great Exhibition of the Works of Industry of all Nations' was, in effect, the first world fair. And as initiator and host of the event, Britain proclaimed itself the world's pre-eminent nation.

> The 'Great Exhibition of the Works of Industry of all Nations' was, in effect, the first world fair.

More than 30 industrial countries accepted the invitation, sent by Prince Albert, to display their materials, machinery and products. France booked an area larger than its entire 1849 Paris Exposition in which to showcase its exquisite 'art manufactures' and much else besides. Exhibitors paid no rent and did not sell their products – this was not a trade fair. Rather, the purpose of the Great Exhibition was to encourage commercial cooperation and free trade between nations. Albert sincerely hoped that through intelligent diplomacy and events such as this, armed conflicts between nations could be banished forever.

Britain's growing confidence

Thanks to naval supremacy and the Duke of Wellington's final defeat of Napoleon at Waterloo in 1815, Britain had emerged from the Napoleonic Wars as a world superpower. That did not mean that it did not have its problems at home. Since the late 1700s the population had been growing at 10 per cent or more a decade. Rural and urban poverty, spreading city slums, epidemics and street crime all seemed to worsen by the year. As Britain's economy stagnated in the years following the wars, some thought the whole country would be dragged down into poverty, disease and starvation.

Yet the worst had not happened. Britain's farms had kept pace with the growing numbers of mouths to feed. Under pressure from social reformers, successive governments were beginning to introduce much-needed reforms – by 1850, laws had been passed on the employment of children and women in factories and mines, outlawing the worst excesses; more men had the vote than ever before (although the franchise was far from universal); new model prisons were being built. And charities sprang up to help the desperately poor.

TEAM EFFORT
The construction of the Crystal Palace in just eight months was only made possible through the cooperation of vast numbers of suppliers, sub-contractors and a team of 2000 construction workers on site. This photograph, taken shortly after completion, brings together some of the men involved. The two on the cross beam were iron fitters, with the task of joining together the thousands of cast iron pieces that made up the frame of the building.

The boozy, licentious William IV was gone, replaced by a young queen in 1837 who had married, quickly produced three heirs, and was living a happy, virtuous family life with her beloved Prince Albert and their growing family. Colonial expansion brought wars and disturbances abroad, but at home there was peace. While 1848 had seen revolutionary turmoil across the nations of Europe, from France to Hungary and Poland, Britain had remained stable.

At the start of the 1850s, Britain had the largest empire the world had ever seen, with a British Navy twice the size of any rival. Bolstered by a mighty merchant fleet and burgeoning industries, the country had overcome the economic instability that followed the Napoleonic Wars to become the richest and most powerful commercial and industrial nation in the world. The Great Exhibition perfectly expressed the nation's confidence and optimism.

The Prince, Paxton and 'King' Cole

The idea of inviting international exhibitors may have come from Henry Cole, the larger-than-life Assistant Keeper at the Public Record Office. Nicknamed 'King' Cole by the press, he seems to have embodied the Victorian version of Renaissance Man. In addition to reorganising the national archives, editing journals and writing books for children, he was passionate about design, especially in manufacturing. He won an industrial design award himself for a practical, elegant tea service, and was also involved in creating the Penny Black, Britain's first postage stamp. As a member of the Royal Society for the Encouragement of Arts, Manufactures and Commerce (the RSA), Cole launched the RSA's exhibitions in 1847 and was keen for Britain to rival the Paris Expositions.

'We must have steam, get Cole' was one of the ponderous Teutonic jokes Prince Albert is said to have enjoyed repeating when he needed someone to move a project forward. Creative organiser Cole and the indefatigable Prince were the driving force behind the Exhibition. Victoria had married Albert, her German cousin, in 1840. Albert was reserved, serious and not entirely at home with English. He could not shake off his unpopularity with both press and people, although government ministers had come to respect him. Albert had been well educated in science, mathematics, art and literature, and to him English education

MAKING PLANS
The Royal Commission for the Exibition (below) was set up at the invitation of Queen Victoria, following a suggestion from luminaries of the RSA. The committee was headed by Prince Albert, who took a hands-on approach to organising the event.

One of Albert's closest collaborators on the project was Henry Cole (above). Cole was an inspired choice for creative organiser of the exhibition, as he was probably the best-qualified man in the country for the task.

The design for the building itself – the Crystal Palace – came from Joseph Paxton (right), master gardener and architect. His design was inspired by glasshouses he had built for his patron, the Duke of Devonshire, at Chatsworth House.

was hopelessly one-sided – English universities and public schools majored on the Classics; science and maths featured only in Scottish universities. He made it his mission to promote science and art education, in order to bring style and good design to Britain's technologically advanced but often graceless products of industry. To this end, he became a member, then President, of the RSA.

> 'It is a grand period in our history when a Prince … is engaged in doing all he can to foster the arts of peace.'
>
> Joseph Paxton

Mindful of his royal role and potential press hostility, Albert had resisted involvement in the exhibition at first, but he agreed to meet Henry Cole and other RSA luminaries on 30 June, 1849, to discuss it. At that meeting he suggested arranging the exhibition around four large themes: Raw Materials; Machinery and Mechanical Inventions; Manufactures; and Sculptures and Plastic Art. His idea was welcomed and this finally persuaded him. It was proposed that the Queen be asked to set up a Royal Commission, headed by the Prince, to plan the event.

FROM DRAWING BOARD TO REALITY

Behind the scenes, Albert threw himself into the project. Before the Royal Commission had even met for the first time, he set about raising interest abroad and backing at home. In the Victorian spirit of *laissez faire* and free trade, the exhibition was to be self-funding and subscriptions were invited from everyone from the Queen downward. A few were generous – some City bankers, including Thomas Baring and a brace of Rothschilds, each gave £500 (about £40,000 today). The then Governor of the Bank of England, in contrast, was derided for his miserly donation of £50 (about £4,000).

At first, money was slow to accumulate. True to British tradition, the press, opposition MPs and more conservative citizens derided the whole idea. Opposition came from all quarters: doctors wrote to *The Times* warning of epidemics of cholera and plague brought by foreign visitors. Clergymen feared foreigners would open brothels in Kensington and spread venereal disease. Undeterred, Albert travelled up and down the country giving speeches emphasising the positive role of technology in engendering social harmony. Time passed and *Punch* chortled over 'blank subscription lists'. But eventually, the money began to trickly in, and then, suddenly, Britain went exhibition crazy. Temperance societies vied with working men's clubs and women's sewing bees to raise the largest subscriptions. Meanwhile, demand for floor space exceeded all predictions.

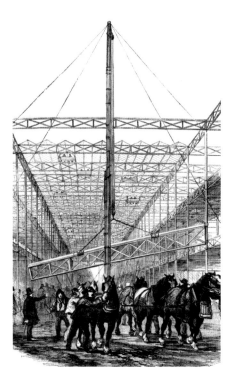

RAISING THE STRUCTURE
The Crystal Palace was one of the first buildings to be constructed using prefabricated cast-iron sections made off-site. This enabled it to rise from the ground with extraordinary speed. The design was only agreed in mid-July 1850, but by late September the main upright columns had been raised. The engraving above shows a girder being hoisted into position in the central aisle, with the help of a team of heavy horses. By December, the four great wooden arched transept ribs were in place atop the third tier. The photograph (right) shows the nave and intersection of the north transept during the building's reconstruction at Sydenham in 1852. Paxton designed glazing wagons (below) to run backwards along grooves in the roof guttering, enabling the 80 glaziers to install 19,000 panes, each measuring 49 x 10in (124 x 25cm), in just one week.

Paxton's glasshouse

As late as the end of June 1850, no one knew where that floor space might be. All 245 designs submitted for the exhibition building had been rejected by the Royal Commission sub-committee charged with choosing a design. As a last resort, the sub-committee – which included the London builder Thomas Cubitt, Charles Barry, architect of the rebuilt Houses of Parliament, and railway engineers Robert Stephenson and Isambard Kingdom Brunel – had published its own design, but that was widely ridiculed as looking like a domed railway shed.

At the last minute, Joseph Paxton submitted a design based on the huge tropical greenhouses he had constructed for the Duke of Devonshire at Chatsworth, Derbyshire, where he was head gardener. The sub-committee would have rejected that as well, but Paxton had given a drawing of his simple, elegant, glass building to *The Illustrated London News*. It was published on 6 July with an editorial calling for its acceptance. The Royal Commission asked Paxton for a detailed tender; the following week, the contract was his.

Paxton's design met all the Royal Commission's requirements for the building. It was cheap – it cost about £80,000 (£6.5 million today). Its prefabricated modules of wrought iron, infilled with glass panels, meant it could be erected quickly. The structure also made it easy to dismantle, an important consideration

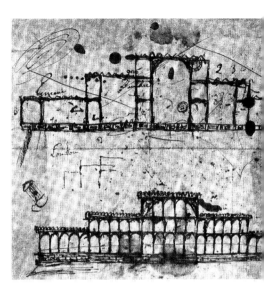

REALISING THE DREAM

Paxton's original sketch (left) was made on a sheet of blotting paper in the boardroom of the Midland Railway in Derby, as late as June 1850. When finished, the building occupied a 26 acre (10.5 hectare) site to the south of the Serpentine in London's Hyde Park (below).

The building was supported on 1074 8 inch (20cm) iron columns. It had an overall length of 1848ft and width of 408ft (563 x 124m). With the upper floors, it offered a total of 991,857sq ft (92,144m^2) of exhibition space. The overall height of the nave was 64ft (19.5m), while the central domed transept rose to 108ft (33m) to accommodate some of the park's stately elms. The building contained 4500 tons of iron, 60,000cu ft (1700m^3) of timber and a total of 293,655 glass panes, measuring 900,000sq ft (83,610m^2).

as Hyde Park, the chosen site, had to be restored to pristine condition when the exhibition was over. Finally, the materials could be re-used: they were to be incorporated into a larger palace at Sydenham, southeast London.

By late September, the upright columns had been raised in the park against a frenzy of objection in the press: the exhibition would spoil the character of the park; visitors would destroy the grass; ancient elms would have to be cut down. The Royal Commission answered every complaint: Paxton added a domed transept to accommodate the threatened elms; the building was supported on iron columns held by large pipes, so deep foundations were not needed. Opposition dissipated as the palace rose at speed, the upper levels begun, without scaffolding, while the lower were still being built. A winter hailstorm disproved the prediction of George Airy, Astronomer Royal, that the building would collapse in a storm. When builders of decorative suburban houses, disapproving of Paxton's minimalist approach, predicted that crowd movement would bring the upper galleries crashing down, a test gallery was built; 300 workmen ran and jumped on it, then a detachment of Royal Sappers and Miners marched across it in step. It stayed up.

The Crystal Palace was built on time and came in below budget. By 31 December, 1850, the main structure was up; by the end of March 1851, the building was finished; by May the exhibition was underway.

INSTALLING THE EXHIBITS
One of the earliest photographs of the Crystal Palace shows carts laden with boxes, delivering goods for display. The nature of early photography gives the image an air of stillness that probably belies the actual situation, which must have been closer to the chaotic bustle of the engraving (left), showing French crates being shipped by rail. With some 100,000 exhibits from around 14,000 exhibitors, getting everything into the exhibition hall and put on display in time was a feat of organisation that rivalled the building's construction.

THE OPENING CEREMONY
A detail from a painting of the opening ceremony shows the Queen, the Prince of Wales and Princess Victoria centre stage, with Prince Albert on the right of the dais. The Archbishop of Canterbury is on the far left of the picture. A Chinese ship's captain who was mistaken for a visiting Chinese dignatory features prominently on the right.

Queen Victoria had followed the progress of the building with great interest and she continued to be a huge fan of the exhibition. She returned time and again and is said to have visited every exhibitor.

A PARTY FOR ALL

Nine state coaches made their way to the Crystal Palace on 1 May, 1851, bearing the royal family, the Court and foreign royalty. After the opening ceremony at noon, the Queen and her retinue proceeded on a royal walkabout. The European royalty present, acutely paranoid since the 1848 revolutions, thought the lack of security reckless. But the Queen recorded her impressions of a 'magical and impressive' building, filled with visitors and a choir which, to the accompaniment of Henry Willis's technically advanced organ, sang Handel's 'Hallelujah Chorus'.

'Here was an occasion which might be celebrated by the whole human race without one pang of regret, envy or national hate.'

The Times, 2 May, 1851

NATIONS ON DISPLAY
A photograph of the eastern nave, which accommodated 6556 foreign exhibitors, with their national flags flying over their displays. The exhibition had 7381 British and Colonial exhibits, making a grand total of 13,937 exhibitors. The dominions and colonies brought colour and romance to the British section: a long delicate birch-bark canoe hung over 'Canada'; a grandly robed stuffed elephant bearing a howdah (canopied seat) towered over 'India'.
And there was always a queue waiting to gaze on the most exotic exhibit of all: the Koh-i-Noor diamond, which had been given to Britain when the Punjab became part of the Empire.

The Crystal Palace was cathedral-shaped, with a nave and transepts. The British and colonial exhibits occupied the western half of the nave and foreign exhibits the eastern end. At the central crossing was a 27-foot-tall (8.2m) pink crystal fountain made of 5 tons of glass by Osler of Birmingham. Fountains played along the central avenue and in the transepts. One, belonging to Johann Maria Farina of Cologne, sprayed eau-de-cologne into the air. There were no deodorants on manufacturers' product lists in 1851 and visitors gratefully saturated their handkerchiefs in Farina's fountain to mask the smell given off by the crowds of thousands on the hot summer days. But there were some mod cons: the palace was uniquely equipped with the first public flushing toilets.

Museum of advanced technology

Like a mighty symbol of industrial power, a gigantic hydraulic press used to make supports for railway bridges loomed above the British machinery section. Visitors stared in astonished silence at the huge steam hammer built by Scottish inventor James Hall Nasmyth, capable of forging great ships' anchors. Also on display was

AN EXCITING DAY OUT

Mr & Mrs John Brown arrive at the Exhibition. Mrs B. had no idea they could have carried it, to such a length. She despairs of ever getting through it.

They are carried in by the crowd.

THE VISITORS' EXPERIENCE

A contemporary cartoon tracked the visit to the exhibition of a fictional Mr and Mrs John Brown, poking good-humoured fun at all the visitors from out of London. Taking advantage of the recently built railway network, the exhibition was the first event of its kind to attract a mass audience from all around the country and from all classes of society. The price of entry came down drastically after the first few weeks to enable as many as possible to attend, and the railways offered special fares to bring the exhibition within most people's reach. An estimated 1 million people visited on the special excursion days – a record 109,915 on 9 October – many of whom had never travelled further than a neighbouring town or village before, let alone to the capital. Rural clergy arrived with smock-wearing parishioners, a teacher herded barefoot ragged-school pupils. There were shiploads of sailors and horse-drawn coachloads of factory workers.

To the horror of *The Times* and some MPs, foreigners arrived in their hundreds by boat from Europe and even North America. But the press commented favourably on the irreproachable behaviour of 'shilling day' visitors. For some – like the Browns – the experience must have been overwhelming. Finding accommodation was almost impossible – visitors overflowed guest rooms in London and for miles around. Many slept out in the open. Perhaps some, like the Browns, found a cab driver who let them rest in his cab, before taking them back to the station in the morning.

A party of Esquimaux, Indians, &c seize a Tub of Tallow, and have a great feast!

Mr & Mrs B, and family, visit a Theatre.

Being oppressed with the heat, they erect an impromptu Wigwam in imitation of those, they see about the Park.

Not being able to find sleeping accomodation at the Hotels, or Lodging Houses, they make themselves as comfortable as they can, in a Cab for the night, with orders to be driven to the Station for the first Train in the morning, having had enough of LONDON & the EXH.

a complete coalpit head, steam-driven fire engines by Merryweather of London, and the Great Western railway's 1847 steam locomotive 'Lord of the Isles'. The textile industries, the drivers of Britain's growth, displayed their advanced machines, some powered by steam turbines that were housed in a separate iron-and-glass shed outside the palace. The latest in steam-driven agricultural machinery was nearby, alongside blocks of Welsh coal used to stoke steam boilers. In the 'Civil Engineering' section was a scale model of Liverpool Docks with 1600 fully rigged ships. But not everything was forward-looking. Two decades after Britain's abolition of the slave trade, the unacceptable side of free trade was evident in the city of Birmingham's range of shackles, manacles and fetters for export to American slave states.

Inspired, exotic and wacky

The electric telegraph and a portable fax machine were among the inventions on display. To the Victorians they must have seemed no more nor less credible than products that seem mad to us today: a 'Silent Alarum Bed' that ejected the sleeper at the set time, or, in the American Court, a coffin guaranteed to prevent decay. Henry Cole's ideal of marrying technical wizardry with design excellence was realised in the Wedgwood galleries, which displayed a machine that reduced sculptors' work to scale. A 'Patent Ventilating Hat' (with air valves) attracted attention among the bombazines, silks, laces, furs and feathers in the textiles section. Textile sub-sections displayed garments from around the world – from latest fashions to tribal costume to utility wear. The neo-Gothic style that we think of today as Victorian could be seen in Augustus Pugin's much-visited Medieval Gallery with its ecclesiastical atmosphere and glowing, jewel-like colours. Minton made the tiles for Pugin's jardinières and won the Commission's Bronze Medal for its boldly glazed majolica-ware.

> ### 'Whatever human industry has created, you find there …'
> Charlotte Brontë

In the exotic foreign displays surrounding the Crystal Fountain, visitors to 'Persia' were excited by reproductions of items found by Austen Henry Layard during his recent excavations of Nineveh, capital of ancient Assyria. On show in 'Egypt' were 165 books, including the first books printed in Arabic, by the Boulac Press, one of the region's oldest printing works. A magnificent throne inset with gems enthralled visitors to 'India'. The Chinese did not send anything, so to save face the organisers assembled an assortment of items from public and private collections in Britain. As if in apology for this imperial oversight, a pigtailed Han Chinese man appeared at the opening ceremony and prostrated himself before the throne. Assumed to be an envoy from the Celestial Empire, he was politely shown to a place among the dignitaries; he was later identified as the captain of a Chinese ship moored on the Thames.

The Queen is said to have adored the tableaux of stuffed rabbits and other animals – some as if at a tea party, others in a schoolroom – displayed by the Zollverein, a customs union of small German states. But art critic John Ruskin was scathing about the quality of the 'fine art' on show.

HIGHLIGHTS OUT AND IN
Among the large machinery on display was this movable steam-powered corn threshing machine and seed drill, photographed here in Hyde Park (top left). One of the biggest attractions indoors was the exotic India room, featuring a magnificent throne encrusted with jewels (left). And crowds constantly milled around the scantily draped 'Greek Slave' (above), by American sculptor Hiram Powers.

FACES OF RECONSTRUCTION

HAND-CRAFTED AND HAND-BUILT
Among the interior displays in the Crystal Palace when it was reconstructed at Sydenham, in southeast London, were massive casts of the colossus of Ramses the Great, reproducing those built by the pharaoh of ancient Egypt at Thebes. There was also a Great Sphinx, shown here (left) being restored.

Reconstruction of the Palace was a massive project, creating a building even larger than first time round. Again, thousands of workmen were employed. In the couple of years since the building had originally been erected, photography had moved on and the second construction was recorded for posterity by pioneer photographer, Philip Henry Delamotte. These two images of workmen on the site were taken in 1853–54. Several of the men are wearing a 'wide-awake', a felt hat with a broad brim and low crown which was popular with workmen at the time.

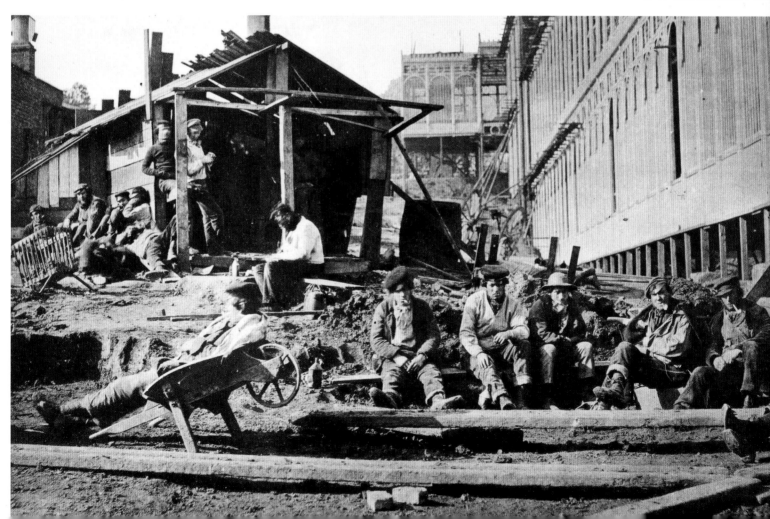

Counting the profits

The cavernous divide between rich and poor, town and country, was a visible problem in 1850s Britain and the organisers were determined to make the exhibition as accessible as possible. From 24 May, Monday to Thursday, tickets were 1 shilling (about £4), and railway excursion trains delivered an estimated 1 million rural and provincial visitors on 'shilling days'.

In all, more than 6 million people passed through the Great Exhibition between 1 May and its close on 15 October. It made a profit of £186,000 (about £15 million today). The money was used to build the South Kensington complex of museums and colleges, including the Science Museum, the V&A and the Natural History Museum, and to establish scholarships and bursaries that are still awarded today. The exhibition boosted international commerce and launched Britain as a tourist destination. But among its exhibits, a discerning eye might spot technologies that would eventually tip the scales of international trade and contribute to Britain's later decline. Essen steelmaker Alfred Krupp exhibited a 4300lb (1952kg) steel ingot cast in one piece – twice the size of the casting exhibited by Britain's steel city, Sheffield. And the Americans showed off a .36 caliber Colt revolver, more reliable than any weapon Britain produced, and the first mechanical reaper by Cyrus Hall McCormick.

PLEASURE PALACE
The Crystal Palace was rebuilt in Sydenham in southeast London. This is how it looked one sunny day in about 1855, with fountains shooting to the sky and people promenading on the broad avenues. Before long the district would be known by the name of its famous new building. The palace remained in use for decades, but was destroyed by fire in 1936.

FASHION

By contrast with the light, shift-like dresses of upper class Regency women, Victorian fashions concealed and restrained the body to achieve a look of modesty and irreproachable morality. Dropped shoulder seams restricted arm movements, making women unable to lift or carry much. Flirtatious Regency hats were replaced by demure bonnets. Hands were tightly gloved. Corsets restricted breathing and movement was further curtailed by the sheer weight of it all – a complete outfit of corset, camisole, petticoats, dress, collar, belt, boots and shawl could weigh a stone (6kg) or more.

CHANGING HATS
By the second half of the decade, prim bonnets tied with broad ribbons were giving way to stylish hats perched on top of the head. Ringlets were a popular hair style.

THE WELL-DRESSED WOMAN
Tiny waists and wide flouncy skirts were typical of the 1850s. Bodices were boned and curved down to a point at the front to emphasise the waist. Evening dresses had a 'bertha' – a low-cut, off-the-shoulder neckline – but day dresses were high-necked with detachable collars. Sleeves were elaborate and often worn with 'engageantes', false undersleeves of white linen. Large, brilliantly coloured pashminas or Paisley-patterned shawls were draped gracefully over a day dress to go out.

In 1856, an American called W S Thomson patented a skirt-shaped frame of wire hoops that could do the job of all but one of the six or more heavy petticoats needed to hold out a wide skirt. The crinoline had arrived. It proved popular because it was light and made walking easier, but dressing still had its difficulties, as this photograph shows (right).

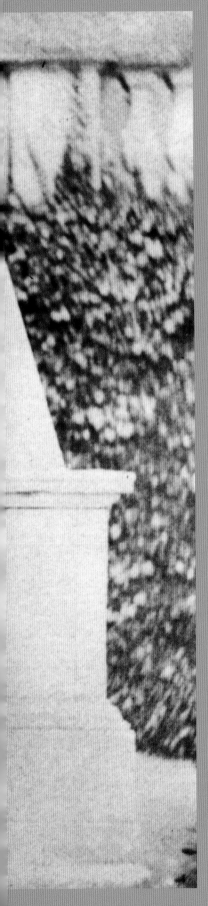

THE WELL-DRESSED MAN

Well-off men wore different outfits for morning, visiting, sports, dinner and club. Compared with Regency fashions, men's clothes were emphatically masculine. Good-quality woollen cloth in sober colours were the hallmark of a gentleman; immaculate tailoring pulled the shoulders back and emphasised the waist. Coats were straight and high-buttoned. Formal frock coats became appropriate business wear in the 1850s. Trousers (known as 'unmentionables') were tubular, perhaps with a military stripe down the side. Shirts were made of linen or cotton. They were plain, white, with starched cuffs and separate, stiff collars, winged for formal occasions, and worn with a cravat or a broad necktie in a bow. For informal occasions, the lounging jacket, single-breasted and short, with rounded fronts and flapped pockets, was becoming popular. Men grew long side whiskers and moustaches and finished off with the top hat – *de rigueur* for formal wear at any time of day. Opera hats folded flat for storing under the seat at the theatre.

CHILDREN'S CLOTHES

Girls and boys from good families wore loose skirts and pantalettes until they were four. Girls then changed to dresses and hats in similar styles to those of their mothers, but with shorter skirts and pantalettes. Boys generally wore skeleton suits – high-waisted trousers that buttoned into a short, tight-fitting jacket. Sailor suits became popular for boys after the young Prince of Wales was photographed dressed in one. Teenagers wore the same style of clothes as their parents.

DRESSING IN CHARACTER

It was considered inappropriate for a maid to dress or wear her hair in a style similar to that of the woman she worked for. The ideal was to be a 'pattern' person – to conform to what was considered correct and appropriate, not to express one's individuality or personal taste through clothes. Details of dress described in Victorian novels were essential clues that enabled people to 'read' characters by their clothes.

To be a well-dressed Victorian was to be appropriately attired for your social and financial status, age and the occasion.

WORKSHOP
OF THE
WORLD

By the middle of the 19th century, Britain's industrial revolution was booming. Having begun around the mid-18th century, it had steadily built momentum: now Britain was entering the second, mass-production stage of industrialisation, decades ahead of any other nation. And yet the military surveyors who were mapping Britain for the Ordnance Survey in the 1850s were surveying what was still overwhelmingly a rural, agricultural country.

LEVIATHAN The *Great Eastern*, built by Isambard Kingdom Brunel and John Scott Russell (in top hat), was by far the largest ship of its day.

THE IMPORTANCE OF FARMING

In the West Midlands, industrial development blighted large swathes of the country, as Queen Victoria discovered on a journey in 1852 that took her through the industrial Black Country. She noted in her journal: 'One sees nothing but chimneys, flaming furnaces…with wretched cottages around them… [the life] which a third of a million of my poor subjects are forced to lead.'

Birmingham's 'flaming furnaces' were producing what were known as 'toys' – small metal goods, arms, trade goods for the colonies and trinkets. The workshops of nearby Wolverhampton were tin-plating and japanning (lacquering), and making the nation's locks and keys – the Queen appointed John Chubb of Wolverhampton as the royal lockmaker in 1847.

Industrialisation also rudely intruded on the rural landscape around London (shipping and engineering), Cardiff (coal) and across Lancashire, where the damp climate favoured the cotton industries – moisture strengthens cotton, so the thread does not break. Drier Yorkshire was the seat of the woollen industries, as well as coal and ore-mining; Scotland's central lowlands were also important for textiles and coal. But away from the sites of industry, its mark could be hard to spot: the northeast had a concentration of shipbuilding and coal-mining, but between its coal pits County Durham remained stolidly rural. Sixteen of England's 39 counties were almost entirely agricultural, and almost half the population of England and Wales still lived in the countryside and small country towns.

In the 1850s, Britain still grew 95 per cent of the food it consumed.

High Farming

By 1850 Britain had the most efficient agriculture in the world. Over the previous century much of it had been restructured, its technology updated, its workforce slimmed down. The result was that larger farms were now worked by fewer people. Iconic characters of the early agrarian revolution, such as 'Turnip' Townsend and Jethro Tull, had introduced root crops for winter cattle fodder and selective breeding to improve meat and milk yields. Horse-drawn seed drills and hoes had increased crop production.

The sleepiest agricultural counties had been scarcely touched by the changes, but in general the new farming methods had crept from village to village across the country, driven by the relentless increase in demand for food from the fast-growing city populations. Since 1800 alone, Britain's population had grown by 75 per cent. The changes had brought prosperity to most farmers, but there was a price in increased hardship and poverty paid by farm labourers and their families. Declining numbers of jobs brought unemployment and homelessness to many, and put downward pressure on the wages of those still in work. Some had formed wrecking gangs in earlier years to target the machines they blamed for taking their

LIFE ON THE LAND A gentleman-farmer in top hat photographed on his well-kept farm in 1857. The picture was taken by William Grundy, one of his studies of rural life published in Grundy's 'English Views'.

FORWARD-LOOKING FARMER
The Scottish agriculturalist James Caird (1816–92) published a treatise on farming in the new era of free trade, entitled 'High Farming as the Best Substitute for Protection'. First published in 1849, it advocated increased use of scientific methods and technology. It was highly popular and brought Caird to the attention of Prime Minister Robert Peel, who sent him to Ireland to report on the country's recovery from the famine.

jobs, such as the steam threshers, invented in the north, which were now speeding up the harvesting of crops in the south. Many farm labourers were forced to become economic migrants and found work – often higher-paid – in the mines, mills and workshops of the industrial areas.

The changes in farming had been effective: in 1850 the UK was still growing 95 per cent of the food it consumed. And still there were calls for more. In 1849 a Scottish farmer called James Caird published a pamphlet calling for more use of new technology and intensive techniques in what he called 'High Farming'. Three years earlier, in 1846, the government had repealed the Corn Laws and the tariffs they imposed on imported grain, and farmers feared cheap food imports. Caird's call to fight off foreign competition by increasing production fell on sympathetic ears. The Royal Agricultural Society, founded in 1838, staged agricultural shows around the country to publicise 'scientific' farming and the farmers responded. Many changed to mixed farming, raising grain and root crops alongside cattle, sheep and pig-rearing. Some great pedigree breeds – such as Aberdeen Angus and Hereford – were established at this time. And mechanical ploughs and threshers, drawn by horse or powered by traction engine, came more into use.

The model farm

In keeping with the move to 'scientific' farming, the 1850s became the era of the 'model' farm. More than a hundred large, 'planned' farms were built, designed not by architects working for rich estate owners, such as the estate farm of Thomas Coke of Holkham in Norfolk, but by agricultural engineers commissioned by

farmers planning for scientific farming. They built power houses to supply steam and water-driven farm machinery, and even tramways to minimise haulage effort. There were purpose-built animal houses with loose boxes, good ventilation and drainage, and central covered yards sloping down to drains. For their owners, such model farms were a huge investment in a promising future.

Some investments made during the 1840s had paid dividends quickly. The Rothamsted Experimental Station was the world's first agricultural research institution, founded in Hertfordshire in 1843 by estate owner and fertiliser manufacturer John Bennet Lawes. His research chemist, Joseph Henry Gilbert, tested fertilisers and their effects on crop growth. Together, they developed nitrate and potassium fertilisers and a method of making superphosphate fertilisers from bones. As farmers began to understand the science behind fertilisers, their use increased and imports of guano – a powerful natural fertiliser from sea-bird droppings gathered in Peru and various Pacific islands – rose dramatically.

Road to market

Carts piled with farm produce clogged the roads into the towns on market days. London – the world's largest city in 1850 with a population of more than 2 million – was supplied daily by its surrounding market gardens, which covered 15,000 acres (6000 hectares) and stretched for 10 miles around. Growers made the journey by night in their carts and wagons in order to reach the markets very early in the morning. In summer soft-fruit sellers hauled loads of strawberries, redcurrants and gooseberries. Autumn markets were flooded with damsons, pears

FRESH FRUIT AND VEG
A normal busy morning at Covent Garden market in London, *c*.1850, as baskets of fresh produce are brought in. The need to increase food production inspired many inventors in the 1850s. John Fowler had been driven to find ways to reduce the cost of food since a visit to Ireland during the famine. In 1858 he won a prize from the RSA for his steam-powered plough, seen in action below around 1860.

CALEDONIAN CATTLE MARKET
Drovers still herded animals into cities to supply meat. In London live animals were sold at noisy, smelly Smithfield, just to the west of the City – still a renowned meat market today. The Metropolitan Cattle Market in Islington (left) – known unofficially as 'Copenhagen Fields, because it was built on the site of Copenhagan House, a former tea garden – was opened in 1855 by Prince Albert. The site was chosen because of its proximity to Kings Cross station, which opened in 1852. There were pens for cattle, sheep and pigs, and slaughter houses nearby. Four huge public houses stood at the corners of the rectangular market – The Lion, The Lamb, The White Horse and The Black Bull. The clock tower in the photograph still stands, overlooking Caledonian Park.

and apples. Norfolk Beefings were in high demand – they were the cooking apples deemed best for apple cake, dumplings and dried apple rings.

Some of Britain's finest roads led to London, and Britain had the best roads in Europe thanks to developments by engineers like John McAdam and Thomas Telford. By the 1840s some 20,000 miles of road had been laid by the turnpike trusts, commercial companies who charged a toll for use of their roads. (The name 'turnpike' derives from the pikes, or spikes, inserted into the top of the toll gates to prevent people jumping over them to avoid paying.) The new roads had made an astonishing difference – the journey time for the London–Edinburgh coach came down from ten days or more in 1750 to just 42 hours by 1832. But good as they were, it was not the roads that revolutionised food delivery. Dry foods like wheat, as well as coal and other heavy goods, were carried on the canal system, virtually complete by 1830. Now, perishable goods such as fruit, vegetables, milk and meat could be express-delivered to the cities by the railways.

THE RAILWAYS

INSPIRED ENGINEERING
Isambard Kingdom Brunel, the visionary engineer of the Victorian era, was a major player in the expansion of the railways, designing viaducts, bridges and the Great Western Railway. Controversially, he opted for a broad gauge track for the Great Western: it made the ride at speed smoother and more stable, but it did not match other main lines being laid at the time, and the choice was heavily criticised by another great railway pioneer, George Stephenson. Brunel (second from right) is shown here at the first, unsuccessful, launching ceremony of the *Leviathan* on the Thames. He is flanked by fellow engineers John Scott Russell (left) – his partner in the venture – Henry Wakefield (centre) and Lord Derby (far right). The ship was renamed the *Great Eastern* after it was sold to the Great Eastern Ship Company.

In 1829 a public competition, known as the Rainhill Trials, was staged by the Liverpool and Manchester Railways Company to find the best railway engine. To enter, George and Robert Stephenson and Henry Booth had to send their 'Rocket' locomotive to Liverpool by ship. In 1832 there were just 166 miles of railway in England; by 1851 this had risen to 6802 miles. The 'Rocket' won the Trials by pulling a carriage with 20 passengers for 70 miles (113 kilometres) and reaching a speed of 29 miles an hour. In 1850 Isambard Kingdom Brunel's 'Great Britain' set a new rail speed record of 78 miles an hour.

The first railways were built to carry coal from mines in the Midlands, the north and Wales to supply the rising demand for steam power. But the railways

tapped into an unpredicted passenger market: rail travel was faster and cheaper (in second or third class) than horse-drawn coaches, and delays were far less likely than on the overcrowded roads. By 1845 the London–Birmingham line had an undreamed-of 1 million passengers a year and the railway companies were making twice as much profit from passengers as from freight.

Building railways was expensive and took years. It involved Acts of Parliament to buy long tracts of land, demolition of buildings in the way, the levelling and draining of land, building embankments, bridges and viaducts, and boring tunnels through hills. The London–Brighton line, with three long tunnels and a viaduct, cost £2,634,059, or £57,262 per mile (today, £175 million and nearly £4 million per mile). 'Railway mania' had gripped the nation during the 1830s and 1840s. Thousands bought shares in companies set up to finance expansion – £125 million (£8 billion today) was raised in the 1840s. As a result, by 1850 the main trunk lines connecting England's major cities and industrial areas were laid and the

> ## In 1850 Brunel's 'Great Britain' set a new rail speed record of 78 miles an hour.

network was being filled in with feeder and cross-country lines, sidings, stations, bridges, even docks, such as London's Poplar Docks which opened in 1852 as a goods terminus for the London, Midland and Scottish Railway. Robert Stevenson's Britannia Bridge, built to carry the London–Holyhead railway over the Menai Strait, opened in 1850, and the Saltash Bridge, designed by Brunel, in 1859. London's Kings Cross Station opened in 1852.

Thomas Brassey – the railway king

Britain exported railways to its Empire. India's first freight railway opened in 1852 at Roorkee in modern Uttaranchal, some 80 miles north of Delhi, and in 1853 a passenger train ran the 21 miles from Bombay to Thana. Both were built under the supervision of British engineers. But the iconic figure in the export of Britain's railway expertise was Thomas Brassey, the 'railway king'.

Born a farmer's son near Chester in 1805, Brassey started as an apprentice to a land surveyor. He met Thomas Telford while surveying the Shrewsbury–Holyhead

THE RAILWAY AGE
By 1850, the main lines connecting Britain's major cities and industrial areas were complete, providing a network carrying passengers and freight. This GWR 4-2-2 broad gauge locomotive was photographed at Swindon Station, Wiltshire, in 1850. The railways inspired major feats of bridge-building. The Royal Albert Bridge at Saltash, named after the Prince Consort, carried the Great Western Railway over the Tamar into Cornwall. The bridge was Brunel's last great project. Brunel died shortly before it was opened, by Albert himself, in 1859. Crowds gathered on the river banks and on boats to watch the ceremony (right).

PRECIOUS STONE
A slate boom was in progress in the mid-19th century and North Wales produced most of the slate needed to supply the building industry. At Llanberis (left) and Ffestiniog, shafts or levels were driven deep into the mountainsides, with some workings descending 1000ft (300m) underground. The first railways were built to haul slate, stone, coal and metal ores from quarries and mines to canals and coastal ports for shipment to building yards and factories.

road, and later worked with Robert Stephenson on the Chester–Crewe railway. Brassey had a flair for managing hugely complex projects and by the 1840s he had built around a sixth of Britain's railways. He then crossed the Channel and built half of France's network. At one time he employed an estimated 775,000 men around the world on projects worth over £30 million (£2 billion today). In 1854 Brassey heard of delays in getting supplies through to the 30,000-strong army of British, French and Turkish soldiers who were besieging Sebastopol, in severe winter conditions, during the Crimean War. So his firm, Messrs Peto, Brassey & Betts, sent navvies out to build a railway from the port of Balaklava to Sebastopol. They did the job in six weeks flat and charged the British government at cost.

Brassey's most ambitious contract was Canada's Grand Trunk Railway, stretching 540 miles from Quebec to Toronto. He began the project in 1854 and in 1859 built the tubular, 3-mile-long Victoria Bridge – designed by Robert Stephenson, and at the time the world's longest – over the Saint Lawrence River at Montreal. To supply the locomotives and the materials for the railway and bridge, Brassey built a model factory in Birkenhead, 'The Canada Works', equipped with a library and reading room for his employees.

Brassey and his partners lost money on the Canada railway, but Brassey still died a millionaire in 1870, having built more than 6500 miles of track in Britain, Europe, Asia, Australia, Canada and South America. During the 1850s he also built the Victoria Dock in London, helped Isambard Kingdom Brunel build *The Leviathan* (later called the *Great Eastern*), the largest ship in the world. At the end of the decade he began work on the mid-level sewer beneath central London, part of Joseph Bazalgette's great scheme and Brassey's most challenging commission.

THE AGE OF STEEL

The British Machinery section at the Great Exhibition was always full of visitors crowding around Henry Bessemer's spectacular steam-and-centrifugal machine for separating white, crystallised sugar from molasses. The sugar acquired an adhesive coating of molasses (black treacle) during the refining process. To separate out the crystals, Bessemer spun the sticky mass in a wire cage at 1000 revolutions per minute, then added cold water. 'In 30 seconds,' explained Bessemer in his autobiography, 'the dark sticky mass was like a snowdrift, with its sparkling crystals compactly spread round the revolving basket.'

The steam centrifuge was an idea that came to him while working on a press to extract juice from sugar cane. 'One invention always seemed to lead to another,' he wrote. Bessemer invented literally hundreds of processes, devices and machines. Some – a type-composing machine, for example – failed simply because they were ahead of their time. He invented a method of compressing plumbago dust (English

PROLIFIC INVENTOR
Henry Bessemer was the stereotypical, prolific Victorian inventor. He was born in Charlton village, Hertfordshire, in 1819, and learned to cast metal in his father's type foundry. He is most famous for patenting a new, faster process for turning pig iron into steel. But not all his inventions were so useful. One of his later creations was a cross-Channel ferry with the cabin mounted on a device to keep it horizontal, no matter how much the ship pitched and rolled, so that passengers would not be seasick. The boat was actually built, but it was so unstable and hard to steer, it destroyed the pier at Calais on its maiden voyage.

HEAVYWEIGHT HAMMER
All through the 1850s, British industry reverberated with the pounding of Nasmyth steam hammers in workshops up and down the country (left). The young James Nasmyth was so fascinated by steam engines that he spent his Saturday afternoons in an iron foundry learning to build them. By the age of 26 he had set up a tool-making business where he invented a steam-powered hammer that could be lifted high enough to take even large objects on the anvil. He also found a way to control the direction and accuracy of the hammer-blow and patented his invention. Nasmyth hammers were so huge they could forge a ship's anchor, and so precise they could break an egg placed in a wine glass leaving the glass intact. Nasmyth retired in 1856, aged 48.

graphite) to make lead pencils, and a way of embossing velvet using heated rollers. Perhaps inspired by the Crystal Palace's 'magic walls of glass', he devised a furnace for making larger panes using rollers, and sold it to Chance Brothers of Birmingham, who had manufactured the glass for the building. An invention that made him substantial amounts of money for years was a steam-driven method of grinding brass to a powder that could be used in pigments instead of gold.

To help the Crimean War effort, Bessemer took out a patent for a new type of rotating shot. It was heavier, with spiral grooves to add a spin, making it more accurate than the army's cannon balls. But his prototype was rejected because it was too powerful for the cast-iron cannon. So he set to work on a smelting process to produce better-quality iron in large quantities, so stronger cannon could be made. During the 1850s a few hundred furnaces were producing steel in small quantities, mainly for the cutlery and tool industries around Sheffield and Birmingham. Large-scale furnaces produced pig iron – raw iron made by smelting iron ore with coke and limestone in a blast furnace. The problem with pig iron is that it contains 3-4 per cent carbon, which makes it brittle. To make a gun in 1854, wrought iron was used – this is pig iron hammered to make it more malleable and to remove some of the carbon, manganese and silicon.

The Bessemer process

Bessemer describes how, while ill in bed, he hit on the idea of blowing air into the molten iron from below. The oxygen in the air would combust, burning off the carbon, and keeping the temperature up and the iron molten. When he tried it in practice, he found mixed in with the molten iron in the vat were traces of some newly formed material. The process, he realised, had created steel, which has a higher melting point than iron. Bessemer then modified the experiment to see if he could convert iron into steel. The results were spectacular.

> After about 10 minutes, [it] was 'sending up a … stream of sparks and a large white flame. Then followed a succession of mild explosions, throwing molten slag and splashes of metal high up into the air … like a volcano …'
>
> Henry Bessemer, on turning iron into steel

After 1856, when Bessemer patented his process, this dramatic display was repeated countless times a day in the cast-iron works of northern England. Molten pig iron was poured into the egg-shaped converter and air blasted through the base until sparks and flames shot out of the top. When the fireworks died down, the converter was tilted and the steel poured out. The inventor set up the Bessemer Steel Company in Sheffield, where there were ideal conditions for iron and steel

LIVERPOOL DOCKS
Along with London, Liverpool was one of Britain's most important ports. Canada Dock in Liverpool (above) displays a few steamships docked in among the sailing ships. The 1850s was still predominantly an era of sail, but the number of steam-powered vessels was growing.

production: coal and iron ore in the local hills, fast-flowing rivers and long-standing metalworking traditions. He licensed the converter to other companies to mass-produce steel – the earliest converter made about 15 tons an hour. Within two years Bessemer was in profit. By 1870 he was a millionaire.

Demand for iron and steel rocketed: they were needed not only for guns and cannon, but also for structural components in bridges and buildings, and for the railways, which by 1850 used more iron than any other industry. Cylinders for steam engines and those unspectacular but critically important machines that make the tools that make machines could all be forged more accurately from steel.

The importance of ships
In transport in the 1850s, shipping soared over roads and railways. Britain's long, corrugated coastline is pierced by navigable rivers and dotted with ports. Small ships could carry heavy and bulky goods around the coasts and up rivers to the cities. In 1855 some 3 million tons of coal were moved by sea to London, compared with 1.2 million by rail. Not surprisingly, Britain was the world's largest shipbuilder and shipbuilding her largest industry, and yet it still operated on a small scale using traditional woodworking techniques. This was the era of the graceful wooden sailing ship – more than 150 were built in Sunderland, the leading shipbuilding region, in 1850. Sailing ships outnumbered steamships by 200 to 1. But change had begun.

In 1837 Isambard Kingdom Brunel had launched the passenger steamer, the *Great Western*, which in effect extended his Great Western Railway to New York. Built of wood, with paddle wheels augmenting the sails, it was the world's largest steamship and the fastest. It cut the transatlantic crossing by more than half, to 29 days. In 1845 Brunel launched the even larger *Great Britain*, the first ocean-going, iron-hulled, screw-driven steamship. In 1851 Tyneside shipbuilder Charles Mark Palmer built the first of what would be many iron-hulled, screw-propelled

continued on page 60

IN WORDS AND PICTURES

For more than a century, excise duty on paper, newspapers, pamphlets and books had made reading an expensive luxury, but by 1850 the pressure to get rid of these 'taxes on knowledge' was having an effect. Following a reduction of the stamp duty on newspapers in 1836, total circulation rose from 35.5 million to reach 53 million by 1850; in June 1855 it was removed altogether. At the same time, advancing technology – in printing, photography, telegraphy and transport – and the advent of public libraries made printed information more available than ever before. As a result, literacy rates rose throughout the decade.

MASTER CARTOONIST
The cartoonist George Cruikshank in 1852 (far left). As well as creating topical political cartoons, Cruikshank illustrated works by Charles Dickens.

NEWS AGENT
Paul Julius Reuter (left) was a German journalist who in 1851 founded the world's first news agency near the Stock Exchange in London. Earlier that year, the first submarine telegraph cable was laid across the strait of Dover from Calais, and the telegraph had also been extended from Brussels to Aachen. By the end of the decade Reuter was supplying foreign news to London's daily papers and to leading provincial ones, such as the *Manchester Guardian*, *Manchester Courier* and *Liverpool Mercury*.

COMIC TRADITION
A cover of the popular satirical weekly, *Punch*, from November 1851, a decade after it was founded.

SERIOUS READING
An edition of *The Lady's Newspaper* from 1849 leads with a report on the famine and mass emigration from Ireland. The publication could claim Queen Victoria among its readership.

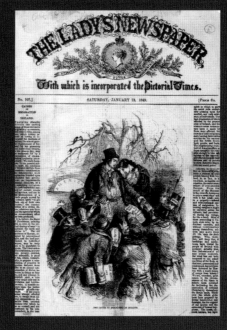

SPECIAL CORRESPONDENT

A new breed of journalist, the war correspondent, was established in the 1850s, consolidating the independence and power of the newspapers in the process. The Crimean War was the proving ground. In 1854, at the start of the war, *The Times* had correspondents in Vienna, Bucharest and Constantinople. William Howard Russell (right) went out to the Crimea itself. Within days of arriving, on 5 April, 1854, he was sending back his 'Letters from the Crimea' for publication in *The Times*.

The correspondents were highly critical of the British military and their inadequate preparations for the war – in comparison, Russell noted, the French had '… even brought machines for roasting and grinding the coffee'. Above all, the news correspondents brought home to the British public the plight of the soldiers. On 12 December, 1854, Thomas Chenery, writing from Constantinople, told his readers of the desperate suffering at the British Military Hospital at Scutari after the Battle of the Alma River. 'What will be said', he asked, 'when it is known that there is not even linen to make bandages for the wounded?'

William Howard Russell began the war accompanying the Brigade of Guards, but his critical despatches soon led High Command to deny him all assistance, including the use of their telegraph. News of the Charge of the Light Brigade, on 25 October, 1854, reached London by telegram; Russell's mailed report was not published until 14 November.

Russell did get to use a telegraph once – to report the fall of Sebastopol. This was the first use of the telegraph by a correspondent from a war zone.

NEWSPAPER READERS

Four out of five of the passengers in this railway carriage of 1850 are shown with a newspaper. By 1855, Britain had 10 dailies catering to a readership of varied political opinions. One was the radical *Morning Chronicle*, which in 1849 commissioned the journalist Henry Mayhew to write a revealing 'Investigation into the Condition of the Labouring Classes of England and Wales'. *The Times* was the leading Tory paper. *The Daily Telegraph & Courier* was launched in 1855, priced just 2 pence – *The Times* cost 7 pence.

There were six Sunday papers ranging from the 'quality' *Observer* and *Sunday Times* to the *News of the World*, launched in 1843 as the world's cheapest newspaper. Even then, the *News of the World*'s mix of news and scandal was a hit: in 1854 its sales topped 100,000 – the highest circulation of any newspaper in the world.

SPACES FOR READING

The British Library reading room (below), under construction in the mid-1850s. The Public Libraries Bill became law in 1850, having been introduced the previous year by William Ewart, both an MP and assistant in the British Museum's Department of Printed Books. The first free public library opened in Manchester in 1852.

RAILWAY CONVENIENCE

The spread of the railways produced a new customer for reading material – the railway passenger, especially those on long journeys. In 1848 William Henry Smith (above) – better known as W H – negotiated an exclusive contract to open a bookstall at London's Euston Station selling newspapers, magazines and books. He then secured deals at stations along most of the new railway lines. As a devout Methodist, he refused to sell any publication that he considered immoral.

NEW NON-FICTION

William Chambers (above) founded the Scottish publishers W & R Chambers with his brother Robert. Their *Chambers Encyclopaedia* was published for the first time in 1859. Another classic reference work, written by a 73-year-old Edinburgh-trained English physician, made its appearance in the decade: Peter Mark Roget's *Thesaurus of English Words and Phrases* was first published in 1852.

TRAVELLING DARKROOM
The Crimean War produced a milestone in photography. In 1855, the photographer Roger Fenton took more than 300 portraits and scenes in the Crimea, creating the first photographic record of a war. His assistant was Marcus Sparling, seen here driving the mobile darkroom that Fenton had specially converted from a wine merchant's van.

HOLD STILL
The long exposures demanded by early photography required subjects to remain quite motionless. This man has been clamped into position with a metal framework to help him keep perfectly still for his portrait.

'I have been working at Inkerman, where my waggon … can be seen by only one of the Russian batteries … It is not amusing at all hearing the whirr of cannon balls approaching.'

Roger Fenton, May 1855, in the Crimea

PIONEERS OF A NEW ART
William Henry Fox Talbot (far left) invented the calotype process, which allowed many copies to be made from one negative. He produced the first book illustrated with photographs, *The Pencil of Nature*, in 1844–46. Frederick Scott Archer (left) invented the 'wet collodion' process, which replaced Fox Talbot's method and remained in use for two decades. Archer earned nothing from his invention as he failed to take out a patent.

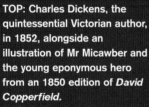

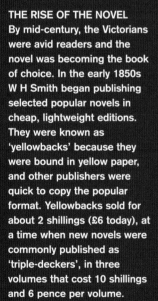

THE RISE OF THE NOVEL

By mid-century, the Victorians were avid readers and the novel was becoming the book of choice. In the early 1850s W H Smith began publishing selected popular novels in cheap, lightweight editions. They were known as 'yellowbacks' because they were bound in yellow paper, and other publishers were quick to copy the popular format. Yellowbacks sold for about 2 shillings (£6 today), at a time when new novels were commonly published as 'triple-deckers', in three volumes that cost 10 shillings and 6 pence per volume.

Despite such high costs, the numbers of new titles grew from around 3000 a year in 1848 to around 5000 in 1853–54. And prices continued to fall: by 1858 the average price of books was 3 shillings and 6 pence.

TOP: Charles Dickens, the quintessential Victorian author, in 1852, alongside an illustration of Mr Micawber and the young eponymous hero from an 1850 edition of *David Copperfield.*

ABOVE: The American writer Harriet Beecher Stowe in 1852, alongside an illustration of Evangeline and Uncle Tom from *Uncle Tom's Cabin*. The novel was the bestselling book of the decade.

TOP RIGHT: William Makepeace Thackeray in 1851, at the height of his renown as the author of *Vanity Fair*.

RIGHT: The prolific Anthony Trollope, who published three of his Barchester novels in the 1850s.

LEFT: Mary Ann Evans, better known as George Eliot, became one of the most revered authors of the Victorian era. Her first novel, *Adam Bede*, appeared in 1859.

steam colliers for the coastal trade to London. But early steamships were prone to break down and in the 1850s the future of steam-driven iron ships was still uncertain.

In 1858 Brunel launched *The Leviathan* (later renamed *Great Eastern*), an enormous ship fitted out to carry passengers in unprecedented luxury, which featured an iron double hull and a four-bladed propeller. The *Great Eastern* was years ahead of its time, not only in size, but in features such as the double hull – a safety measure that the *Titanic* did not have, which is now compulsory. It was impressive in many ways, but it was not a commercial success.

The *Great Eastern*'s size was a problem – it was too large even for the state-of-the-art Victoria Dock, which opened on the Thames in 1855. This was the first Royal Dock, equipped with hydraulic machinery and rail links. The Thames was the hub of imperial trade and a noisy, bustling docking point for trading ships from all over the world. Liverpool came a close second. It was the docking point for African palm oil (used for candles, soap and lubricating machinery), American cotton, tobacco, sugar and grain. Liverpool had expanded its historic docks during the 1840s – in time for the Great Exhibition, whose 'Civil Engineering' section displayed a scale model of the docks with 1600 fully rigged ships.

In Belfast, the precursor to the great Harland & Wolff shipyard was built in 1853 and flourished as the decade progressed under the management of Edward Harland. And in Wales, new docks were built at Cardiff for the burgeoning export trade in coal that was cheap and ideal for use in steam engines. The development of Welsh coal-mining transformed the formerly pastoral Rhondda Valley.

TEXTILES

In 1845 Samuel Cunliffe Lister, a Bradford industrialist, patented a machine to separate and straighten tangled raw wool. Like James Hargreaves before him, who is credited with having invented the spinning jenny in 1764, Lister's title to the invention is questionable. Some say that it was his partner, Isaac Holden, who invented it, just as some believe that Hargreaves' colleague, Thomas Highs, designed the first spinning jenny. And just as research has shown that Richard Arkwright used the patents of other inventors in his 1771 water frame, Lister made use of an earlier patent for combing coarse wools taken out by his associate, George E. Donisthorpe of Leeds.

Historians suggest that the importance to industrial progress of any single invention has been overplayed. Usually, several inventions appeared to speed up processes such as spinning, and they would be improved, adapted to different textiles and modified for new types of power. As their use spread, the industry changed. Once perfected and widely used, the woolcombing machine – whether rightly Lister's or not – transformed woollen cloth-making.

It was the textile industries that made Britain into the 'workshop of the world'. They had spearheaded industrialisation and they were still the power driving the economy in the 1850s, when textile exports grew by more than 25 per cent. So much cotton was needed to supply Lancashire's mills and hand weavers that India, the original source, could no longer supply enough to keep Britain's spinners and weavers busy, and so more and more American cotton ships unloaded raw cotton on to Liverpool's docks. The slave trade may have been banned by Britain, but that did not stop its industrialists taking the product of slave labour. American cotton was cheaper because the slaves were unpaid, and it also had longer fibres, so it produced better-quality textiles.

TECHNOLOGY FOR WOMEN
A sewing machine had been on display at the Great Exhibition. The labour-saving potential of the device was immediately recognised, but the cost was prohibitive for most. This gentleman is showing an interest in his wife's skill with the new machine that would, in later years, pale with familiarity.

HOME WORK
The large mills may have been taking work from home spinners and weavers, but garments were still stitched by hand. Home-dressmaking remained a major source of employment for women – it was one of few ways of making a living that were available to respectable women.

TITUS SALT AND SALTAIRE

A MODEL MILL-OWNER

Titus Salt was one of the most important entrepreneurs and philanthropists of the industrial revolution. He made his fortune in Bradford after inventing a process for weaving mohair and alpaca. In the first half of the 19th century, the burgeoning textile industry led Bradford's population to grow from about 13,000 to more than 100,000. This caused huge problems of pollution and Salt became concerned about the effects on the health of the mill workers, whose average life-expectancy fell to as low as just 18 years of age. Salt tried to introduce anti-pollution measures in Bradford itself, but faced with intransigent opposition, he determined to move his own mill out of the city. The result was Saltaire, a model factory and village that took 20 years to build. The view below shows it from the north.

The site that Salt chose was in a well-known beauty spot on the moors, beside the River Aire and the Leeds and Liverpool canal just a few miles out of Bradford. He set about building his state-of-the-art mill in 1851 (below), and once that was complete he started on houses for his workers. They were architect-designed and stone-built, each with water and gas and its own outside lavatory. There was access to wash-houses, bath houses and a hospital, almshouses for the elderly, allotments and a park. Other facilities he provided included a recreation centre with a library, a reading room, concert hall, billiard room, science laboratory, gymnasium and boathouse, just visible in the foreground.

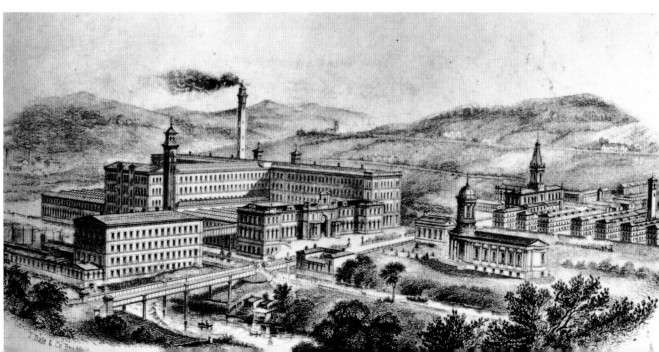

Industrialisation made patchy progress, in uneven stages, and even as late as 1851 the textile industries employed fewer than 1 million people, of whom less than two-thirds worked in mills and factories. In the worsted industry about 50,000 people worked part-time on hand looms in their cottages, supplying local mills by the piece. But by then, hand spinners and weavers in all branches were struggling to survive in the face of the relentless increase in steam-powered mill machines.

By 1850, Samuel Courtauld employed more than 2000 people in three silk mills with steam-powered looms. The French Jacquard loom, which could weave patterns using punch cards without input from the weaver, had boosted silk production in Derby and Macclesfield, and in 1855 Bradford manufacturer Titus Salt made a machine that could spin silk waste into yarn. New technologies had also been applied to the production of linen in Belfast and even stiff and stubborn industrial hemp and jute textile production in Dundee.

Goat wool and alpaca

Expanding trade with the East was bringing exquisite new textiles to Britain's ports – silks, brocades, satins and velvets, and mohair from the Turkish Angora goat. The early 1850s saw a fashion craze for cashmere (also called pashmina) shawls woven from the hair of goats in the Himalayas.

The story goes that in 1831 Titus Salt of Bradford first bought a shipment of wool taken from the long-haired Russian Don goat, but local spinners could not process it. Bradford produced worsteds – wool textiles with a sheen produced by using yarn spun from wool with long fibres that are combed straight. Salt set up an experimental mill and using his knowledge of worsteds, developed a method of spinning 'Donskoi' wool into a soft, silky, mohair-like yarn. It was so profitable that when, two years later, he happened upon a cargo of alpaca, he bought samples. Wool from llamas and alpacas had first reached Britain as ballast in ships returning from South America. Two mills had tried and failed to spin the delicate fibre on their machines, but with his knowledge of Donskoi wool, Salt was able to produce a light, strong yarn that made a lustrous fabric fine enough for gowns.

NEW AND IMPROVED
Manufacturers were constantly striving for ways to improve their yarns. This advertisement for Meltham Mills near Huddersfield in Yorkshire claims to offer an improved cotton for crocheting. The Brook family had established a small silk mill in Meltham village in the 18th century. By the mid-1800s their cotton mill was the largest in the area, employing hundreds of workers. The Brooks were philanthropic employers, who built houses, schools and a convalescent home for their workers. Edward Brook is remembered today as a patron of the Meltham Mills Brass Band.

A FORWARD-LOOKING ERA

Most technical advances in the textile industry came by trial and error, or accidental discoveries, but university-trained chemists were soon applying science to the evolution of chemical processes such as soap-making and bleaching. The most spectacular advances in industrial chemistry were made in the dyeing industry during the 1850s. In 1852 a student at the Royal College of Chemistry (an institution nurtured by Prince Albert, established in 1845 to aid industry) produced the first synthetic dye.

While experimenting in his parents' garden shed, seeking to make synthetic quinine from coal tar, William Henry Perkin accidentally extracted a reddish-brown sludge. The discovery had already been made in 1846 by a French chemist,

Frédéric Crace Calvert, who was appointed Professor of Chemistry at the Royal Institution in Manchester, but it was Perkin who spotted its potential as a textile dye. He found it had a rich purple colour and called it 'mauveine'. The 1850s saw a rash of new purple dye discoveries: murexide was synthesised from the uric acid in guano in 1853, and French Purple ('mauve' in France), was processed from lichens in 1856.

Gas, electricity and other ideas

Black coal mined from underground was the source of the gas that by the 1850s illuminated streets, shops, factories, workshops and houses all over Britain. Meanwhile, a new lighting industry was developing in response to Michael Faraday's experiments with electricity. In 1848 engineer William Staite had flooded the portico of the National Gallery in London with light from innovative new lamps, and he designed parts of the arc lamps on display at the Great Exhibition. A decade later, the South Foreland Lighthouse became the first to be equipped with an electric light – an arc light with a steam-powered generator, set up with Faraday's help.

Many future technologies would grow out of scientific discoveries made during the mid-Victorian era. In 1834 John Scott Russell, a future working partner of Brunel and one of the organisers of the Great Exhibition, observed a wave on a canal in Hermiston, near Edinburgh, as it formed then travelled forward when horses pulled a canal boat to a halt. Fascinated, he spent decades investigating what he termed 'waves of Great Translation'. Such waves are now used in fibre-optic communications as stable pulses of light, called solitons, that carry large amounts of information. In 1851 William Thomson, a Scottish mathematics professor, worked out the basis of electrical oscillation, which would lead to the discovery of radio waves. And in 1854 an Irish mathematician, George Boole, published *An Investigation of the Laws of Thought*, in which he explained his ideas for substituting symbols for all words used in logic. Today's computer arithmetic is based on his boolean algebra.

ADVANCED DESIGN
An early design for a helicopter by English inventor Sir George Cayley. Recognised by many as the father of aeronautical engineering, his 3-part paper entitled 'On Aerial Navigation' (1809-10) revolutionised aerodynamics.

Important concepts for fibre-optic communications and computer arithmetic emerged in the scientific thought of the 1850s.

The first manned flight

Some 70 years after the Montgolfier Brothers had invented the hot-air balloon, a Yorkshire baronet and amateur aeronautical engineer called Sir George Cayley built a large glider with a scientifically efficient wing. The craft flew across a Yorkshire dale in 1853, with his coachman as the unwilling pilot. This is believed to be the first manned heavier-than-air flight.

One particular bad habit that reached Britain in the 1850s was cigarette-smoking, introduced by Crimean War veterans who had learned to roll their own with black tobacco from their Turkish allies. Philip Morris, a tobacconist, began to sell hand-rolled cigarettes along with pipes and cigars in his London shop in 1854. Two years later war veteran Robert Peacock Gloag set up Britain's first cigarette factory in Peckham, South London, feeding crushed Turkish tobacco into tissue-paper cylinders and packaging them as 'Lucky Threes'. Just two years later, *The Lancet* medical journal published the first of what would be many readers' discussions of the health effects of smoking.

SCIENTISTS

LEFT TO RIGHT AND TOP TO BOTTOM:
1. George Cayley (1771–1857), British scientist and aeronautical engineer.
2. Michael Faraday (1791–1867), English chemist and physicist, holding up a glass bar used in his experiments.
3. James Young (1811–83), Scottish chemist and founder of the paraffin industry. He patented a method of distilling paraffin oil and wax from shale, which enabled production on a commercial scale.
4. William Fairbairn (1789–1874), Scottish engineer who invented the riveting machine, which speeded up constructions with wrought iron. It was used for the iron girders of the Britannia Bridge in Wales, which had a span almost twice as long as

any bridge built before. He also invented a new steam boiler with twin flues and furnaces, which improved performance.
5. Charles Babbage (1792–1871), English mathematician credited with early work on the world's first computer.
6. Charles Darwin (1809–82), English naturalist who first formulated the theory of evolution, published in *The Origin of Species* in 1859.
7. George Boole (1815–64), Irish mathematician, logician and philosopher. His Boolean algebra, invented during his tenure as professor of mathematics at Queen's College, Cork (now University College), is now fundamental to the field of computer science.

QUEEN AND CONSORT

The arranged marriage between Victoria and her cousin Albert blossomed into a partnership based on genuine love and mutual respect. Victoria came to depend on him for help and advice in matters of government, and she gave him the female devotion he had not known as a child. They shared a happy family life, with nine children who all grew to adulthood, and became the model family for the nation.

CONTENTED QUEEN Victoria, photographed in 1854, holding a portrait of her beloved Albert.

A UNIQUE RELATIONSHIP

The Duke of Wellington, hero of Waterloo and Commander in Chief of the Forces, was 81 on 1 May, 1850, and ready to retire. Earlier that year he had visited Windsor and suggested to the Prince Consort that Albert should take over command of the army. This was an extraordinary turnaround in the Duke's opinion of the Prince. Ten years before, when still a Tory MP, he had accused the Queen's German husband-to-be of 'papalistic' sympathies and ordered him to declare himself a Protestant. The Duke and his fellow Tory MPs had even managed to reduce the income allocated to the young Prince. But a decade of Prince Albert's dedication, calm courtesy, discretion and common sense had convinced not only the Duke, but also most government ministers, of his loyalty, sound judgment and formidable capabilities.

Albert turned the Duke's offer down. Before his wedding in 1840, this prince from the diminutive Duchy of Saxe-Coburg and Gotha had been given the honorary British title of field marshal, but he had no military experience. Now the press had got wind of the possible appointment and headlines were asking whether the army of the British Empire would want a Saxon prince at its head. But the Prince's main consideration, he stated in his reply to the Duke, was whether the position would interfere with his role as consort to the Sovereign 'and the performance of the duties which this position imposes on me.'

A most unusual job

Back in 1840, Albert had confronted the main dilemma of being royal consort to the British queen: the role has no job description other than to sire heirs to the throne and be the Queen's escort. Unlike a British aristocrat, Albert could not buy a seat in Parliament or hold political office. Effectively, he had no job. For an intelligent 20-year-old, educated by some of the great minds in European learning and bursting to use his position to benefit both his adopted country and Europe at large, this was an intensely frustrating position to be in. Albert had to create his own job. It became clear to him, he told the Duke, that his duty was to 'entirely

FROM PRINCESS TO QUEEN
A self-portrait of Victoria, shortly before her accession to the throne on 20 June, 1837, aged just 18. Her upbringing was very sheltered, and almost entirely in the company of women – notably her mother and her governess, Baroness Louise Lehzen. Victoria was crowned Queen of the United Kingdom of Great Britain and Ireland on 28 June, 1938. The image below, from a painting by Franz Winterhalter, shows her taking the sacrament during her coronation in Westminster Abbey.

sink his own individual existence in that of his wife … make his position entirely a part of hers …'. His task was to assist the Queen with the burden of work that her position entailed, and to put his powers of observation and analysis at her service, so that she might become even stronger than a male monarch.

Putting these ideas into practice proved to be a struggle. Prince Albert had no official status since Parliament had denied him a peerage, which would have given him a vote in Parliament and a seat on the Privy Council (the body that advises the monarch). The Queen had requested that he be made King Consort, but the Prime Minister, Lord Melbourne, refused to consider it. Albert was not even allowed to choose his own German private secretary. With Victoria's approval, Melbourne appointed his own former secretary to the Household and selected the Gentlemen to attend the Prince.

Even worse for Albert was the Queen's unwillingness to let him take part in political affairs. The constitution barred him from signing state papers, but Victoria would not allow him to read any and avoided even discussing politics with her husband, arguing that he had no deep understanding of British contemporary history and affairs. Albert, mature and patient beyond his years, was conciliatory, promising to study them in depth. Then he busied himself with public responsibilities and networking to try to improve Britain's unimpressive record of education in science, technology, art and design, and he patronised the new London Library. In 1840 he was appointed President of the Anti-Slavery Society, for which he made his first public speech in English

The Queen's contradictions

Victoria adored her handsome husband, an athlete who excelled at fencing, and deplored his humiliating constitutional position. In her journal she railed against the 'infernal Tories', who had cut his annuity from an expected £50,000 a year (about £3 million today) to £30,000. 'You Tories shall be punished', she wrote. But Victoria knew that on her accession in 1837 the government had been relieved to be rid of the Hanoverian kings – the Georgians – some of whom had been notoriously licentious, profligate and costly. (As a woman, Victoria could not inherit the crown of Hanover, which the Georgians had shared with Britain.) Parliament was reluctant to bestow power upon another impecunious prince of a minor German state. Victoria also knew that the idea of having another foreigner influencing policy was just as unpopular with the public as it was with Parliament.

For all her adoration of Albert, Victoria herself harboured some resentment at his enthusiasm to involve himself in her monarchical duties. She

continued on page 73

THE QUEEN MOTHER
Victoria's mother was Victoria Maria Louisa, the Duchess of Kent, a daughter of Franz Frederick Anton, Duke of Saxe-Coburg-Saalfeld. Her marriage to the Duke of Kent – George III's fourth son, Edward – was her second, her first husband having died in 1814. She was also the aunt of Prince Albert, which made Victoria and Albert first cousins.

Albert believed his role was to 'sink his own individual existence in that of his wife' so that she might be a stronger monarch, he told the Duke of Wellington.

END OF AN ERA – THE PASSING OF THE DUKE

'He was, beyond all doubt, a very great man …'

Charles Greville, Clerk to the Privy Council and political diarist

PORTRAIT OF A DUKE

The Duke of Wellington (left) was 75 when this rare daguerreotype was taken of him by Antoine Claudet, a celebrated French photographer, in 1844. Wellington was the hero of the nation, with a most illustrious past behind him. He had won victory after victory in India, Spain and Portugal, and ultimately, in 1815, had defeated Napoleon at the Battle of Waterloo. And he still had no intention of retiring. After serving as Prime Minister from 1828 until 1830, he had been reinstated as Commander in Chief of the Forces in 1842. He served in Robert Peel's second administration and was Leader of the House of Lords.

Wellington was also Chancellor of Oxford University and had numerous lesser titles and occupations. He overworked and often complained about it: 'Every other animal – even a donkey – is allowed some rest, but the Duke of Wellington never!' A series of minor strokes left him deaf in one ear, but his infirmities did not diminish his attraction for society ladies. He enjoyed balls and country house parties and was often seen walking arm in arm with lady friends in St James's Park. Throughout his seventies and into his eighties, he was greatly admired, even revered: 'He is followed like a show wherever he goes,' commented Charles Greville. He was a frequent guest at Balmoral, and the Queen had visited him at Walmer Castle in Kent, his residence as Warden of the Cinque Ports.

It was at Walmer that Wellington died, at half past three in the afternoon of 14 September, 1852. He was seated in his favourite wing chair, with his son, daughter-in-law and trusted servants around him. His body was embalmed, death masks were taken and casts of his hands were made in bronze. Locks of his silver-white hair and even his false teeth were given to relatives as mementoes. He was laid in a coffin of mahogany, encased in outer coffins of pine, oak and lead. On 9-10 November, some 9000 people queued on Walmer beach to file past the coffin before it was carried under escort by train to London.

The funeral took place on 18 November, 1852 (below). More than a million people stood in respectful silence as the cortège, headed by the enormous funeral car – designed by Prince Albert – travelled from Horse Guards to St Paul's Cathedral. On his final journey, the Duke was escorted by 3000 slow-marching infantrymen, eight cavalry squadrons, Chelsea pensioners and a private from every regiment in the British army. A groom led the Duke's horse. Prince Albert's coach-and-six headed the mourning coaches, but the Queen sent an empty carriage. Victorian protocol forbade ladies from attending a funeral and Victoria, moved to tears, watched the procession from the Buckingham Palace balcony. 'Britain's pride, her glory, her hero,' she declared in her journal.

'[This event] may be said to have surpassed in significant grandeur any similar tribute to greatness ever offered in the world.'

The Illustrated London News, 20 November, 1852

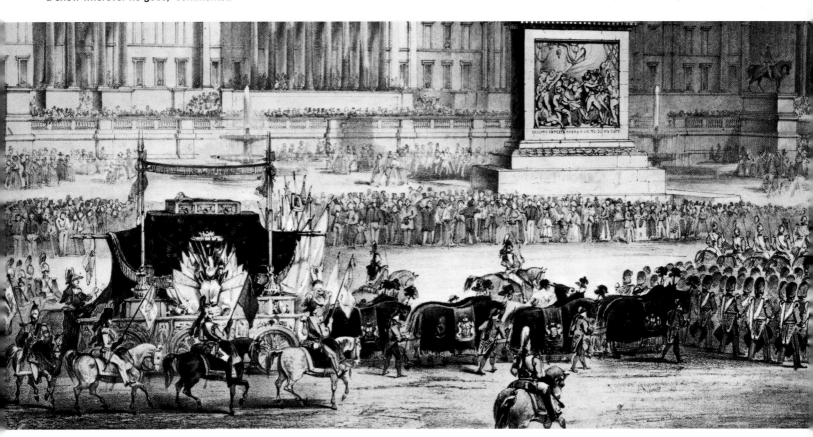

had spent her teenage years closely closeted with her mother and governess, never allowed friends or a moment's solitude. She had now had three years of independence on the throne – and found she enjoyed it. So although she valued her marriage and loved her husband, she wanted to keep them in a separate sphere. Initially, she failed even to involve Albert in issues in which her prime minister Lord Melbourne and, later, Sir Robert Peel advised her to include him.

THE V&A PARTNERSHIP

Luckily for Albert, Victoria soon became pregnant. In case the Queen should die before the child reached majority, Parliament designated Prince Albert as Regent, giving greater weight to his constitutional status. Increasingly fatigued by pregnancy, Victoria allowed Albert to read to her from the government despatch boxes she received each day. Soon he was selecting which papers to read. Before long, he was penning notes to the Prime Minister and Foreign Secretary for her to sign. On 21 November, 1840, the day their first child, Victoria, was born, the Prince Consort represented the Queen at a Privy Council Meeting.

By the birth of their third child, Alice, in 1843, Albert was effectively manager of the Queen's affairs, her informal secretary and chief adviser. He accompanied her at audiences with ministers, received copies of documents and drafted replies in her style of writing. She so clearly relied on him that ministers would at times consult Albert before approaching the Queen. By 1857 he had so immersed himself in political affairs that the Queen sometimes complained of seeing too little of her husband: 'I have the rare happiness of being alone with my beloved Albert', read one day's entry in her journal that year.

Political realities

In the early years of the marriage, Victoria made little secret of the fact that she preferred Lord Melbourne and his Whigs (Liberals) to the Tories. But Albert believed that monarchy should be above party politics, and that the Queen's open support for the Whigs was not in her interest. He persuaded her to be more objective towards the Tories, and in so doing he developed an understanding with Robert Peel (prime minister 1841–46), who discussed with him the major questions of the day – the Corn Laws, free trade and reforms to relieve poverty.

When she came to the throne, the Queen had little appreciation of the poverty of most of her subjects. Furthermore, Melbourne misrepresented social reform proposals to her, suggesting that professional agitators were behind them, so in 1846 she refused to support Lord Shaftesbury's Ten Hours Bill to reduce working hours in mills and factories. Peel made the royal couple more aware of the facts. The Prince visited a London slum and became President of the Society for Improving the Conditions of the Labouring Classes. He met Lord Shaftesbury and supported his housing schemes. On a visit to Parkhurst Prison, the Queen was horrified to see child prisoners.

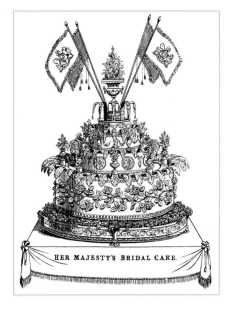

HER MAJESTY'S BRIDAL CAKE.

MATCH MADE IN HEAVEN
Victoria and Albert first met in 1836, when Albert visited England with his father and older brother, Ernst, and met the Princess at Kensington Palace. They met again in October 1939, when the two brothers came once again to England to pursue the match. The couple were engaged the same month and married on 10 February, 1840, although not everyone was as happy about the match as the couple themselves. They were ideally suited and very happy together, so much so that more than a decade and several children later, when the Queen agreed to be photographed in 1854, they re-enacted the wedding for the camera (left). Victoria's elaborate gown is embroidered with flowers and edged with lace.

THE PRIVATE FACE OF ALBERT
Albert came across as reserved and serious in public, but those who knew him well found him good company. Both Albert and Victoria were immensely fond of music. On one occasion, in 1842, the German composer Felix Mendelssohn played for them in private.

Improving education

In 1849 the Prince Consort was elected Chancellor of Cambridge University, an honorary position that nevertheless gave him a platform for the reform of higher education. A Royal Commission was appointed in 1850 to look into Oxford and Cambridge, and quickly instigated far-reaching changes. New study areas were approved in 1851, including science, engineering, philosophy, law, history, theology and European and oriental languages. In 1855 university entrants were no longer subjected to religious tests and a year later Roman Catholics and Dissenters were admitted as undergraduates.

Victoria recognised that her own education had been less than adequate to prepare her for monarchical duties. She had studied scripture under an Evangelical clergyman; history, French, German, Italian and arithmetic with her governess, Baroness Lehzen; and singing and dancing. Later, a tutor taught her some natural philosophy and literature. Albert helped her to fill the gaps, reading aloud on religion, politics or history, explaining science and taking her to see Shakespeare, concerts, ballet and opera, which she loved.

'King to all intents and purposes'

By the 1850s, Queen and Consort had forged a working partnership to deal with the demands of the State and those of their European relatives. The diarist Charles Greville, Clerk of the Privy Council, noted as early as 1845 that 'as he likes and she dislikes business, it is obvious that while she has the title, he is really discharging the functions of the Sovereign.'

The monarchy in Britain had changed over the 18th century as the Hanoverian kings relinquished powers to the government. The constitutional monarch now had, as the Victorian essayist Walter Bagehot summarised, 'the right to be consulted, the right to encourage, the right to warn', but must ultimately accept the decisions of prime minister and cabinet. In 1851 the Whig Prime Minister, Lord John Russell, resigned after losing the vote on a franchise reform Bill, but the Tories could not form a government. The Queen, after taking advice, formally asked Russell to return to power. Had she not succeeded in resolving this constitutional crisis, the monarchy's prerogative to call upon a minister to form a government at such times might have been lost to Parliament.

But the Prince had no constitutional right to be 'King to all intents and purposes,' as Greville described him, and the V&A partnership had to tread carefully. At times they overstepped the mark. Having discreetly turned down the role of army commander in chief in 1850, Albert allowed himself a link with the army, which desperately needed to modernise, by appointing himself Commander of the Grenadier Guards. The position came with a small salary – and large heaps of press condemnation. In 1850 the press denounced his lack of objectivity towards any government policy that adversely affected members of his family in Saxony, particularly Coburg. Albert asked himself in a memo why monarchs were denied the right to have political opinions.

> 'Albert grows daily fonder and fonder of politics and business, and is so wonderfully fit for both ... and I grow daily to dislike them more and more.'
>
> Victoria, in a letter to her uncle, King Leopold of Belgium

DEPEND ON ME
A photograph taken in 1854 (right) seems to capture the essence of the royal couple's relationship. Albert is the caring, constant husband at the Queen's side, offering support and advice.

LISTEN AND LEARN
Albert did everything he could to promote science in Britain and supported the foundation of many scientific bodies, such as the Royal Institution of Great Britain. He is shown here seated in the front row at a lecture given at the Royal Institution in December 1855 by the inventor and scientist Michael Faraday. The Prince is flanked by his two eldest sons, Edward and Alfred, respectively the Prince of Wales and Duke of Edinburgh.

Foreign affairs

One area where the royal couple did have influence over government affairs was in foreign policy, and their views often clashed with those of Lord Palmerston, Foreign Secretary in Lord John Russell's government of 1846–51. Victoria and Albert wanted their government to oppose movements that threatened their relatives on European thrones. But Palmerston openly supported groups striving for independence, such as the movement struggling for the unification of Italy, which threatened the make-up of the Austrian Empire (a significant part of what is now Italy was then under Austrian rule). While Albert was working behind the scenes for a unified, liberal German state, Palmerston supported Denmark's claims to the German duchies of Schleswig and Holstein.

Palmerston was a master of tactics. He sent despatches to foreign governments without submitting drafts for royal approval, or failed to include amendments requested by the Queen. She was enraged by his behaviour. She and the Prince regularly corresponded with European heads of state, she insisted, and had to deal with their complaints about Palmerston's actions. But it was Palmerston who bore ministerial responsibility – and who had his finger on the nation's pulse.

Poor public relations

Both Palmerston and the people disliked the suppression of Italian and Hungarian independence movements by the Austrian Empire. In 1851 an exiled Hungarian revolutionary, Lajos Kossuth, was given a warm welcome on a visit to Manchester and Palmerston announced his intention to receive him. The Queen protested to the Prime Minister. Later in the year, Palmerston resigned. Palmerston's supporters blamed Albert and his influence upon the Queen. The fact was that after more than a decade in Britain he had not managed to endear himself to the public. He still had not lost his 'foreignness' – though he spoke English well, it was not with accent-free fluency. Those who knew him found him engaging, down to earth, kind, even humorous, but in public he embodied the qualities the British traditionally attributed to the Germanic character: he appeared reserved, formal, humourless and too intellectual, and was a gift to press cartoonists. To the drinking, gambling, womanising aristocracy he seemed prudish and awkward.

'You will scarcely credit that my being committed to the Tower was believed all over the country …'

Albert, in a letter to Baron Stockmar, 4 January, 1854

The success of the Great Exhibition of 1851 temporarily transformed Albert's image. His profile was further enhanced when the profits were declared. 'Albertopolis' was the popular name for the 87-acre (35-hectare) site for museums and colleges in South Kensington, paid for from the Exhibition's proceeds. Yet the goodwill quickly evaporated. The military appointments he made as Commander of the Grenadier Guards failed to impress. Again he found himself the butt of attacks for meddling in foreign policy. In 1853, as the country moved towards war

A ROYAL VISIT
The engraving below records a visit by Victoria and Albert to Leeds in 1858, to open the new town hall. The Queen's popularity, if not the Prince Consort's, was high by the 1850s. She was given a rapturous welcome by the crowds, which *The Times* described as 'one long sustained outburst of loyal enthusiasm'.

in eastern Europe, Albert took a cautious stance and, in a wave of xenophobia, he was accused of being pro-Russian. The same year Palmerston briefly resigned after a disagreement with the Prime Minister over a proposed Reform Bill. Although he was quickly reinstated, Albert was blamed for the resignation. The rumblings erupted into a crisis early in 1854 when broadsheets appeared in the streets trumpeting the news that Albert had been arrested and taken to the Tower of London. Crowds gathered there, agitated and murmuring, waiting for Albert and Victoria to appear. The Queen eventually asked the Prime Minister to denounce the lies in Parliament and MPs rallied in Albert's support.

Further hostility was overtaken by Britain's declaration of war on Russia. During the extraordinary atmosphere in the build-up to the Crimean War, the Queen stepped instinctively into her patriotic role, echoing the bellicose sentiments of her people – and of Palmerston, who had wanted to take a hard line with Russia much earlier. Victoria followed the progress of the hostilities closely, feeling the pain and ecstasies of pride and loyalty in her country.

In 1857 Queen Victoria asked Parliament to give her husband the status of Prince Consort. Yet even now, the cabinet again found grounds to object. But Victoria was determined. In June that year, she used her royal prerogative to give Albert the title herself, by Letters Patent.

ROYAL FAMILY LIFE

The Queen gave birth to Princesss Beatrice, her ninth child, in 1857. That same year her first born, Victoria, the Princess Royal, was 17 and became engaged to Prince Frederick William of Prussia. Albert had arranged the marriage as part of his plan to help to create a united, liberal Germany.

The marriage of Victoria and Albert in 1840 had also been a marriage of convenience, but the couple had fallen very much in love. Throughout their marriage they were devoted, faithful, happy and, their biographers record – and the prolific child-bearing indicates – enjoyed a fulfilling sex life. Victoria, who had grown up fatherless, had wanted time to get accustomed to her new husband, yet within a month of her wedding she was pregnant. 'I prayed God night and day to be left free for at least six months,' she confessed in a letter. A year after the birth of the Princess Royal, their first son, Albert Edward ('Bertie'), arrived – the first heir born to a reigning monarch since 1763. By 1850, when their third son, Arthur, was born, the succession was guaranteed.

continued on page 82

MODEL FAMILY
Victoria and Albert with all of their children, photographed shortly after the ninth and last child, Beatrice, was born in 1857. The Queen is seated holding the new baby, with her eldest daughter Victoria, the Princess Royal, standing behind her. Edward, the Prince of Wales, is to the right of Princess Victoria, with Louise (6th child) and Leopold (8th) in front of him. On the left is Alfred (4th child), leaning against the parapet beside Albert. The three in front of them are Alice (tallest, 3rd child), Helena (5th) and Arthur (7th).

FAMILY ALBUM

RIGHT: Albert Edward, later to be Edward VII, with his sister Alice. Edward was always knows as 'Bertie' and despite being the eldest son and heir, he was the black sheep of the family. He hated study and did not respond to any of his tutors – his younger brother, Alfred, was cleverer. His parents despaired of him, but he was probably reacting against excessive parental strictness. Alice was the first of Victoria's children to die – of diphtheria in 1878, aged 35.

BELOW: Queen Victoria was an accomplished artist and often sketched her children when they were young. The group portrait is of the three eldest – Victoria (seated), Edward and Alice. Victoria, the Princess Royal – known as Vicky – was the clever one in the family and grew up to be very close to her father. The bottom sketches are of Arthur, aged 3. They are labelled to show him 'on parade', 'out walking' and 'at home'.

ABOVE: The princesses Helena – known as Lenchen – and Louise photographed in matching tartan dresses in 1856. Louise turned out to be artistic. She studied sculpture and is generally considered to have been gifted. The statue of Queen Victoria overlooking the Round Pond outside Kensington Palace is one of her pieces.

ABOVE RIGHT: A coloured engraving of the royal family at Christmas. Albert introduced the German custom of having a tree decorated with lighted candles as part of the family celebration. When the public heard of the custom, it caught on and the Christmas tree became a British tradition.

RIGHT: Prince Alfred, the second son and Duke of Edinburgh, photographed in a kilt by Roger Fenton in 1856. The fashion for kilts and tartan was copied throughout the country.

A NEW KIND OF ROYAL HOME
Victoria loved to escape from her London palaces. Osborne House on the Isle of Wight (right), photographed in 1857, and Balmoral in the Highlands of Scotland were favourites. The royal couple bought Osborne House in 1844 and Albert re-built it in Italianate style with London builder Thomas Cubitt. The family usually spent time there in early summer. In August Victoria herded them to Balmoral, which she adored. She had the house decorated almost entirely in tartan – even down to the carpets and chairs in the drawing room (above). The royal family's love of tartan became known as 'tartanitis'.

Victoria's pregnancies were dogged by what doctors today might diagnose as post-natal depression, a condition then attributed to 'hysteria'. Victoria, kind and warm-hearted on the one hand, was also stubborn, imperious, with a legendary temper on the other. Entries in her journal, and notes that Albert wrote to her, reveal how she swung from a clinging dependence on him to hostile accusations and rages. After the birth of Beatrice in 1857, her physician warned that another pregnancy might cause a break down. Victoria made repeated efforts to control her outbursts and depressions, and for his part, Albert seems to have employed self-control, sympathy and patience with his wife. But despite such trials, Albert and Victoria derived great happiness from each other and their large family.

It was not to last. Albert was ailing through much of the 1850s, with attacks of stomach pain and biliousness. Retrospective diagnosis shows that his death in 1861 may not have been the result of typhoid, as recorded, but possibly the final stage of cancer. There was no relaxing of duty, however. In 1859 much correspondence was demanded by conflict in Europe and a weakening Austrian Empire. In May Albert opened Brunel's magnificent Royal Albert Bridge across the Tamar and presided over the annual meeting of the British Association for the Advancement of Science. European monarchies, he had always been sure, would wither away if they did not make themselves useful to their people.

THE VICTORIAN FAMILY

Queen Victoria and Prince Albert set the moral tone for the family in the Victorian era. Respectability was paramount, and to be respectable you must do your duty to your family: it was a man's duty to be the breadwinner and an authoritative husband and father; a woman must be an efficient and careful housekeeper, a supportive, obedient wife and a dutiful and watchful mother. Respectable families were practising Christians, expected to attend church and to hold regular family prayers. Children were perceived not so much as miniature adults, as the generations before had done, but as developing individuals who needed to be trained to be responsible and useful, through strict discipline and punishment if necessary.

LEFT: A middle class mother and her young children, photographed in the parlour. Babies and children were fed to a strict time schedule. Most upper-class women gave their babies to a wet-nurse and depended on nannies, governesses and tutors to care for their children. Poorer mothers cared for their children themselves and older girls usually looked after younger brothers and sisters. Ideally, the children of all social classes would be out of the way and the house quiet when father arrived home from work.

BELOW: An upper class family in their garden, getting ready for a game of croquet.

PEASANT LIFE
A country family in the doorway of their cottage, photographed by William Grundy in 1857. Most of their clothes would have been hand-me-downs or homemade – the young woman is knitting, probably with re-used wool.

The barefoot boy would have been one of the 2 million children across the nation – three-quarters of them from poor families – who attended Sunday School.

PLAY TIME
When they got the chance to play, marbles were a popular game with children of the poorer classes, like this group of young boys. Millions of poor children had to go to work at the earliest possible age to contribute to the family upkeep. Poor parents sometimes gave away or sold their children into adoption, labour or, in the worst cases, prostitution.

THE BIG OCCASION
Wedding parties were generally held at home, after a service in church or chapel. Most were simple affairs, but the better off could make the occasion rather grand. This photograph shows guests at the high society wedding of the Reverend Frederick Manners Stopford to Florence Augusta Saunders on 6 August, 1857. Florence was the daughter of Charles Saunders, the first general secretary of the Great Western Railway. Isambard Kingdom Brunel was among the distinguished guests.

MUSICAL AMUSEMENT
Ladies from Queen Victoria downwards were taught to play the piano and sing. Most 'withdrawing' rooms had a piano, and those that did not usually had a pianola – a mechanical piano that played tunes from a paper roll. Hymns, old favourites and the latest songs from popular musicals and operas were sold as sheet music, and many an evening was spent around the piano.

A DAY OUT
Sundays were family days, and increasingly, with the spread of railways, that could mean a day out – perhaps to the seaside, like the women and children enjoying Pegwell Bay, in Dorset, in this realistic painting by Dyce. For those with small children, a new form of transport also appeared in 1850 which made a walk in the park more comfortable for everyone: the perambulator.

In more religious households, Sunday revolved around church and prayers. The morning service would be followed by Sunday School or Bible readings for the children, prayers with the servants, and possibly Evensong as well.

Family life revolved around the drawing room, originally the room where family and guests withdrew from the dining room for entertainment after dinner.

AN EVENING IN
A family taking tea with their guests in 1855.

GOVERNMENT
AND
EMPIRE

In 1850 Britain was a superpower with the largest, most advanced navy in the world, a wealth of overseas settlements, colonies and trading stations, and a mighty merchant fleet plying its trade routes. These needed to be protected from encroachment by rival powers. And the European rival most feared in the middle of the 19th century was Russia. Determination to contain the Russian Empire would lead to an alliance with France and Turkey in the Crimean War.

CRIMEAN WAR COUNCIL A meeting of the British, Ottoman and French commanders – Lord Raglan, Omar Pasha and General Pelisier.

COLONIAL EXPANSION

I n 1850 Britain had the largest empire the world had seen – and it was still growing. St Lucia, Malta, Ceylon and many other places with trading or strategic importance had been won or occupied piecemeal during the Napoleonic Wars. British settlers had taken over new territories such as New Zealand, which in 1852 achieved a degree of self-government, with its own constitution under a colonial governor. The older colonies were growing up. In Australia, Victoria, with 77,000 settlers and about 5 million sheep, was recognised as a separate colony in 1850. South Australia, with wheatfields to feed the booming population of the post-1851 gold rush era, was recognised in 1856.

Price of power

Successive governments leading up to the 1850s were concerned about the cost of administering and protecting their new territories. Nonetheless, in 1847 they supported the founding of a new colony and military base on the uninhabited island of Labuan off the northwestern Borneo coast. Labuan's attraction was coal, which made it a useful fuelling station for ships trading between Hong Kong – recently acquired from China – and British-controlled Singapore.

Often, expansion was driven by people like James Brooke, a colourful English adventurer and former soldier of the East India Company. Brooke had established himself in northwest Borneo in 1841, when he was created Rajah of Sarawak by the Sultan of Brunei. In 1847 he was appointed Britain's governor in Labuan and Consul-General in Borneo. He fought against piracy by the Dayaks, Borneo's tribal peoples, into the 1850s. In addition to their reputation for piracy, the Dayaks were known for taking human heads in war raids.

Westminster's worries about expenditure on colonisation proved justified in 1852, when the empire-builder Lord Dalhousie, then Governor General of India,

continued on page 98

MOTHER OF PARLIAMENTS
The Houses of Parliament in Westminster, viewed from the south bank of the River Thames in 1858. Following a fire in 1834 which destroyed much of the old Palace of Westminster, the House of Commons was rebuilt to a design by architect Sir Charles Barry (right, 1795-1860), the pre-eminent architect of the decade, in collaboration with A. N. Pugin. It was still under construction when this photograph was taken (left).

MISSIONARIES AND ADVENTURERS

MISSIONARIES AND ADVENTURERS

'Providence seems to call me to the regions beyond.'

David Livingstone, 1851

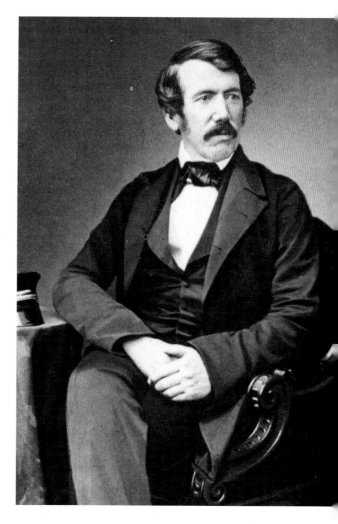

THE COLONIAL MISSION

Some ventured into the colonies for reasons other than profit and trade. Missionaries like Scotsman David Livingstone (1813–73) followed a calling to see 'the smoke of a thousand villages, where no missionary had ever been.' In 1850 his fame was spreading as the first European to see Lake Ngami, in Botswana. This photograph of him (right) was taken in 1852, after returning from exploring the upper Zambezi.

Livingstone not only wanted to found Christian missions, he also hoped to weaken the slave trade by opening up new trade routes across Central Africa. In 1854–5 he travelled across Africa from coast to coast, and on that journey became the first European to see the great waterfall known to locals as Mosioatunya – 'The Smoke that Thunders'. He renamed it Victoria Falls. Back in Britain he was lionised for his achievements and his travels were romanticised in colour (bottom right). Livingstone himself made light of the trials of exploration. In his journal on 12 June, 1852, he noted: 'I have drunk water swarming with insects, thick with mud and putrid from rhinoceros urine and buffaloes' dung, and no stinted draughts of it either, yet never felt any inconvenience from it.'

Livingstone returned to Britain in 1856 and was awarded the Royal Geographical Society's gold medal. He then published *Missionary Travels*, which sold out to an admiring British public thirsty for knowledge of Africa. Another notable Scot, William Ridley, published books on the Aboriginal languages of Australia and formed the Moreton Bay Aboriginals' Friends Society in 1855. Perhaps he and his wife looked like the missionary couple below, surrounded by Aborigines in European-style dress.

English explorer Samuel White Baker (left, 1821–93) was best known for exploring the Upper Nile and discovering Lake Albert, one of the Nile's two great reservoirs. Before venturing to Africa he had spent a decade in Ceylon, now Sri Lanka, where he founded an agricultural settlement in the highlands and encouraged settlers from England to join him. This picture of him was taken in about 1855, the year he left Ceylon.

used a dispute with the Governor of Rangoon over shipping to launch a war that led to the annexation of the Irrawaddy Delta in Burma. The new dependency was strategically important, but it failed to generate the expected income in trade, and was a drain on Britain's finances.

TRADE AND WAR

On the other side of the world, a recurrence of war with America had been expected ever since the War of Independence ended in 1776. Border disputes between the USA and British North America, better known as Canada, flared up from time to time. The Great Lakes had seen battles between American and British troops in a two-year war that broke out in 1812, when the Americans attempted to invade. A treaty of 1818 established the boundary between the two along the 49th parallel from Minnesota to the Rocky Mountains, but beyond that the United States laid claim to all of Oregon Country, encompassing the entire western seaboard all the way north to Alaska. The British wanted the boundary in the western part of the territory to follow the Columbia River.

In 1846 the Oregon Treaty was signed, dividing Oregon Country in two. The frontier was fixed along the 49th parallel, except for a loop to keep Vancouver Island wholly British. The British part (British Columbia) would be controlled by the Hudson's Bay Company until 1858. But the exact line of the boundary south of Vancouver Island was not made clear. In the 1850s a dispute flared over the San Juan Islands that lay between Vancouver and the mainland.

A war about a pig

The Hudson's Bay Company had a sheep station on San Juan, but American farmers had also settled on the island. In 1853 Washington made a formal claim to

FORT VANCOUVER, USA
Originally a British trading post run by the Hudson's Bay Company, Fort Vancouver found itself in American territory after the Oregon Treaty of 1846 extended the western part of the US-Canadian border along the 49th parallel. The US Army set about building a new fort (below) near the site of the original British fort on the northern bank of the Columbia River. Although the Oregon Treaty guaranteed the Hudson's Bay Company the right to continue operating from Fort Vancouver, with free access to the river and the sea, political pressure prompted the company to move north to Fort Victoria in what is now British Columbia.

the area, but in June 1859 events took a hand. A pig belonging to the head of the sheep station got into the garden of an American farmer and ate some of his potatoes. The farmer shot the pig, and the Hudson's Bay Company demanded the farmer's arrest. The American settlers requested military assistance, and US soldiers were sent out. Three British warships then arrived in the harbour, followed by more American soldiers, then two more British ships. Realising that the 'Pig War' could get serious, US President Buchanan sent General Winfield Scott to negotiate with the British governor. The escalation was halted, but the troops remained. The British occupied the island's northern end and US troops the southern until 1872, when the German Kaiser was asked to arbitrate. He decided in favour of the US and the soldiers were withdrawn.

Britain's relations with the USA were rather more productive over the plan to build a ship canal across Central America from the Atlantic to the Pacific. In 1850 the British government ratified a treaty pledging both countries to recognise and respect the neutrality of the future canal. There was confidence in peace, and it signalled a boom in trade. The mood seemed to spread. In 1855, the Governor General of British North America, James Bruce, 8th Earl of Elgin, signed the Canadian–American Reciprocity Treaty, agreeing to free trade in natural resources. On 31 December, 1857, Queen Victoria renamed Bytown, a centre of the Ontario timber trade, as Ottawa, and made it the capital of the colony.

India and the East

India was Britain's largest colony by 1850, still under the control of the British East India Company. Trade was vital, but the wealth of the sub-continent's

ANGLICANS ABROAD
The interior of St Peter's Church in the British East India Company's stronghold of Fort William in Calcutta (Kolkata), photographed in about 1850. It was the practice of colonials to take the trappings of home with them. In matters of religion, they built for themselves places of worship that would not have been out of place in the Home Counties.

COLONIAL CHILDCARE
An Indian nurse, or *ayah*, photographed in about 1858 with her colonial charge fast asleep in her arms. The British administration did attempt to improve the lot of women, in particular that of widows. By Hindu tradition, a woman committed *suti* if her husband died, throwing herself onto his funeral pyre. The British outlawed the practice and tried to make it possible for widows to remarry.

potentates was so overwhelming that control and taxation had become the main motive for Britain's presence there. In effect, the Company had become more an agency of the British state than a commercial organisation, backed by a colonial army to deal with any unrest.

Colonisation of India was still underway. The Punjab had been taken over in 1849, after fierce fighting against the Sikhs. In the north, the once-troublesome Gurkhas – natives of Nepal, an independent state beyond Britain's frontiers – had been defeated, then befriended. In 1856 Britain acquired Awadh (Oudh), a buffer state on the northwestern border, through the 'Doctrine of Lapse' introduced by Lord Dalhousie, Governor General from 1848–56. This had ended the traditional practice by which childless rulers adopted an heir: instead, if a native ruler died without an heir and his line ended, his state passed to the East India Company.

By now, most of southern, western and eastern India was under British control, and there were two British armies present – the troops of the Crown and those of the East India Company. Even so, these amounted to fewer than 40,000 men and British rule relied on some 200,000 Indian troops known as 'sepoys'. These made up the bulk of the Company's army, commanded by British officers trained at the Company's military academy in Surrey.

The Indian Mutiny

In 1857 disaffection with British rule tipped over into full-scale revolt in the Bengal army (see page 102). The immediate spark for the rebellion was the issue of new Enfield muskets, but discontent had been growing in many parts of Indian society. The annexation of large areas of territory caused resentment, and in the army British officers often paid scant attention to the cultural and religious sensitivies of the men under their command. Although British rule was restored, the reprisals wreaked by some British troops – not just on the rebels but on the general population – stoked anti-British feelings even further.

Back in Britain there was profound shock at the uprising. 'We are in sad anxiety about India, which engrosses all our attention', Queen Victoria wrote to her uncle Leopold in Belgium. The government responded promptly to the emergency and in 1858 abolished the East India Company, transferring its powers to the Crown. Lord Canning, Governor General from 1856–58, was made Viceroy. With the support of the Queen, who thought the reprisals of British troops 'quite shameful', Canning adopted a more moderate approach and abandoned the policy of colonial expansion. The army was reorganised and reinforced with more troops from Britain.

'There is not a family hardly who is not in sorrow and anxiety about their children ... India being the place where everyone was anxious to place a son!'

Queen Victoria, in a letter to Leopold I, King of Belgium

continued on page 104

UNDER ATTACK Troops stand by their guns in front of the mosque at the Khynabee Gate, Delhi, during the 1857 Indian uprising against British rule.

THE INDIAN MUTINY

RUMOUR, REBELLION AND REPRISAL
New Enfield muskets, more powerful and more accurate than the old smoothbore Brown Bess muskets, were issued to sepoys serving in the British East India Company's army in 1857. Objections were soon raised over the cartridges, which soldiers had to bite open as part of the loading process. Rumours spread that the paper cartridge cases were greased with pork and beef fat. This was anathema to both Muslim and Hindu sepoys – Muslims did not touch pork fat as they believed pigs to be unclean, and Hindus could not touch beef as they held the cow to be sacred. The alleged use of animal fat on the cartridges was seen as typical of the British disregard for Indian sensibilities – possibly a prelude to enforced conversion to Christianity.

On 9 May, 1857, sepoys of the Bengal Light Cavalry at Meerut refused to use the cartridges, and were stripped of their uniforms and imprisoned. The next day, the garrison erupted as sepoys turned on the British officers and their families, killing many. The mutineers then marched on Delhi, where the Bengal troops there joined them in a rampage against the British.

Four months later the British re-took Delhi, but in June a large rebel force had besieged a few hundred British in Kanpur (Cawnpore), near Lucknow. Eventually, the garrison surrendered and accepted the sepoy leader's offer of safe conduct out of Kanpur. But on 27 June, as the British boarded riverboats, shots were fired and the evacuation went horribly wrong. In the confusion, the boatmen are said to have set fire to the boats. The British men were shot and about a hundred women and children taken hostage. As British reinforcements approached, a rumour spread among them that the sepoy rebels had engaged butchers to hack the hostages to death.

Stoked by such rumours, when the Company troops re-took Kanpur in July they retaliated savagely. They tortured the town's inhabitants, forced pork and beef fat down their throats, and even fired them from cannons. Many of these people had in fact refused to support the rebels and helped the British. Rebellion spread to Oudh, the home state of many Bengal sepoys, where it was eventually subdued in 1858. The uprising was confined to the Bengal army, but it is seen by many as the first phase of India's independence movement.

ABOVE: Hindu Rajput soldiers, photographed in 1857. The high-caste Rajputs were a traditional warrior caste.
RIGHT: Mann Sing Maharajah of Lucknow and a Prince of Oudh, which became a stronghold of the Indian Mutiny the year after its annexation by the British in 1856.
LEFT: In the aftermath of the fighting, rubble strews the approach to the Rumi Darwaza or Turkish Gate (left) in Lucknow in 1858, shortly after the Indian Mutiny. The Asafi Masjid mosque, part of the Bara Imambara complex, can be seen on the right.
BELOW: Lt C H Mecham (standing, centre) and Lt Anderson (seated, right), of the British Hodson's Horse cavalry regiment, photographed in 1857 with Sikh troops loyal to the British during the Indian Mutiny. The regiment was raised in response to the rebellion.

Gunboat diplomacy

In the same year as the Indian Mutiny, Britain went to war with China in what became known as the Second Opium War. The First Opium War had begun in 1840 when Britain's foreign secretary, the charming but arrogant Viscount Palmerston, sent a fleet to blockade Canton (Guangzhou), giving rise to the phrase 'gunboat diplomacy'. The Chinese imperial authorities had always kept a tight rein on trade with Western countries, limiting foreign access to China. They traded tea, porcelain and silks with the British in return for silver, but the price of silver rose dramatically in the 1830s and the East India Company decided to trade another commodity – opium. The use of opium was strictly banned in China, but the East India Company shipped in Indian opium to sell on the black market there. In 1840 the Chinese authorities seized a consignment in the British trading settlement in Canton, and in response Palmerston sent in a force of warships, frigates and state-of-the-art steamships. By 1842 China had been forced to open trading ports to the West and cede Hong Kong to Britain.

The Chinese continued to resist foreign trade, and especially the opium trade. In 1857 they captured *The Arrow*, a British-registered ship trading out of Hong Kong, on suspicion of carrying opium. It signalled the start of the Second Opium War. Britain formed a coalition with France, the United States and Russia to force China to open its doors to them, and they attacked and occupied Canton. In 1860 they took Tianjin, defeated the imperial army, looted the Emperor's exquisite Summer Palace and threatened Peking (Beijing). The Chinese capitulated, agreeing to open up five more ports. They were also forced to pay reparations, cede territory to Britain and Russia, respect religious freedom – and legitimise the opium trade.

The trouble with Palmerston

To the intense irritation of Victoria and Albert, it became increasingly difficult to exert any sort of control over Palmerston's actions in foreign affairs. His gunboat diplomacy went into action in Athens in 1848, after a business belonging to a Jewish trader called Don Pacifico was attacked by an anti-Semitic crowd. Don Pacifico was Portuguese, but he had been born in Gibraltar, so was technically a British subject. When the Greek government denied him compensation, he appealed to Britain to intervene. Without consulting the Queen or the Cabinet – never mind the governments of France and Russia, Britain's allies in guaranteeing Greek independence from the Ottomans – Palmerston sent Royal Navy gunships into the Aegean. The blockade lasted until 1850, when the Navy seized and held Greek ships and property until the government agreed to pay compensation.

The Queen asked Lord Russell, the prime minister, to sack Palmerston, but instead, in June 1850, a censure motion was moved against him in the House of Commons. During a heated debate, Palmerston vigorously defended himself against his critics, accusing them of intrigue and conspiracy and arguing that, like Roman citizens, every British subject should be confident that 'the watchful eye

AFTER THE BATTLE
The Union Jack flies over one of the Taku Forts at the mouth of China's Hai River. British and French forces captured the fort in 1860, during the Second Opium War, opening the way to Tianjin and Peking (Beijing).

and strong arm of England will protect him against injustice and wrong'. The motion was defeated.

Furthering Britain's interests was the keynote of Palmerston's policies. He also strongly believed that the other countries of Europe, where monarchies retained far greater power, would benefit from a system of constitutional government more like Britain's. To that end, he supported movements striving for independence, such as in Belgium and Italy – in 1849 he had secretly supplied Garibaldi's rebels in Sicily with arms for an uprising.

The Queen and Prince Albert were constantly infuriated by the way Palmerston undermined European monarchies – many of whom were their relations. But Palmerston's stance was more in tune with the public. In March 1854 Guiseppe Garibaldi, hero of the Italian independence movement, sailed into the River Tyne aboard *The Commonwealth*, and was given a tumultuous welcome by a working-class crowd at South Shields.

Palmerston overreached himself in 1851 over Louis Napoleon of France. The nephew of Napoleon Buonaparte had been elected president of the French Republic in 1848, but on 2 December, 1851, he seized dictatorial powers as Emperor Napoleon III. The Cabinet agreed to remain neutral on the issue, to the Queen's profound relief, and instructed the British

VISCOUNT PALMERSTON
Beginning his political life as a Tory MP in 1807, Viscount Palmerston gravitated to a Whig-Liberal position. He served three stints as foreign secretary, the last being from 1846–51 in John Russell's government, and was home secretary under Lord Aberdeen when the country went to war in the Crimea. He was prime minister in 1855-58 – this photograph was taken in 1857 – and again from 1859. By the time of his death, in 1865, he was regarded as a symbol of British nationalism.

VICTORIA'S PRIME MINISTERS
John Russell, 1st Earl Russell (left), was the Whig
prime minister from 1846–52. He did not long survive
sacking Palmerston in 1851, but returned to the seat
of power from 1865–66 following Palmerston's death.
George Hamilton Gordon, 4th Earl of Aberdeen
(bottom left) was prime minister in 1852-55, heading a
coalition of Peelites (Tories) and Whigs (Liberals).
Palmerston and Russell were both in his government
when the decision was taken to go to war in the
Crimea against Russia. The other prime minister of
the decade was the Earl of Derby, who served briefly
in 1852, and again in 1858.

ambassador in Paris to communicate this to the French
Government. Meanwhile, Palmerston had conveyed his enthusiastic
support for the new Emperor to the French ambassador in London.
He was forced to resign over the issue by the Prime Minister, Lord
Russell, but soon returned to government as home secretary in a
coalition administration under Lord Aberdeen.

The road to war with Russia

Suspicion of Russian intentions dominated foreign policy. Russia
was the largest of Britain's European rivals and a first-class military
power. In 1828 it had attacked and won territory from the Ottoman
Empire, raising fears of further expansion in the East. Although
Afghanistan's Amir, Dost Mohammad, was anxious to remain on
good terms with Britain, Palmerston believed he had made a secret
alliance with Russia and Persia. So in 1838 Palmerston sanctioned a
disastrous war against Afghanistan with the aim of making it a
buffer state to defend British India from Russia.

The British army under the Governor General, Lord Auckland,
captured Kabul and installed a puppet ruler. Unfortunately, this
ruler was hated by the Afghans, who had already deposed him
once. Outraged, they rose against the British, and in January 1842
forced them to retreat through the mountains in the freezing winter
cold. Harried all the way by Pashtun warriors, just one of some
15,000 British troops plus around 10,000 family and followers
survived the disastrous retreat from Kabul. A relief force later
re-took the Afghan capital, but withdrew after releasing British
prisoners there.

By the 1850s, the question of how to stop Russia taking more
territory from the declining Ottoman Empire was paramount. The
Russians had ports on the Black Sea and Britain was convinced that
they wanted to gain access for their ships to the Mediterranean.
This threatened French as well as British interests. The best policy
seemed to be to shore up the Ottoman Empire, so that it would
remain a buffer state against Russia's expansion southward. So the
old enemies teamed up with the Ottomans and, in 1854, went to
war in the Crimea (pages 108–13).

continued on page 114

THE CRIMEAN WAR

It was fought on the Crimean peninsula, but at the time everyone called it the Russian War, because its aim was to curb Tsarist power. The object was to prevent Russia winning territory from the failing Ottoman Empire that would give its ships direct access to the Mediterranean Sea. The threat was strong enough to bring the old enemies, Britain and France, together on the same side supporting the Ottomans. War was declared in March 1854. The Russians withdrew in September 1855, and a peace treaty was signed in Paris in March 1856.

FINDING THE TROOPS
Despite public enthusiasm for the war in the Crimea, it was not easy to find the troops to take on the Russians. It was almost 40 years since Britain had fought a major war, and the army, under its Commander in Chief, the Duke of Wellington, had been scaled down to just 45,000 men, with no reserves. About 27,000 troops were assembled under Lord Raglan, a 66-year-old one-armed veteran of Waterloo, who had never commanded forces in the field or fought in a modern war.

The troops below are the 57th Regiment under Colonel Shadforth, photographed on the plain of Sebastopol in 1855.

OFFICERS AND GENTLEMEN
Uniforms were extremely varied for British officers serving in the Crimea. These men dressed in an assortment of garments are all officers of the 42nd Highlanders, The Black Watch (right).

The 7th Earl of Cardigan, James Thomas Brudenell (far right), was the cavalry officer in command of the Light Brigade. The celebrated charge against the Russian heavy guns took place during the Battle of Balaklava on 25 October, 1854.

PORT IN A STORM
Winter in the small harbour at Balaklava, through which the British forces received all their supplies. In October 1854 the Russians launched a surprise attack on the British supply base here. Then, on 14 November, a 'Great Hurricane' did even more damage, wrecking 21 ships that carried stores for the winter. The troops had landed dressed in summer uniform and winter clothing had not been issued. Food rations were so meagre that starvation threatened. There was no firewood, no cooking stoves and no fodder for the horses and mules, which weakened and died of starvation. By December 1854 the British army had been reduced to about 13,000 men.

'Mackintoshes, quilts … bedclothes, sheets of tent-canvas went whirling like leaves in the gale towards Sebastopol.'

William Howard Russell, on the storm of November 1854

FRENCH FORCE
A troop of Zouaves, the elite Berber troops of the French army. The Zouaves led the first assault in the Battle of the Alma River in September 1854, during the advance to Sebastapol. The day was eventually won by a spectacular uphill British charge that captured the main Russian artillery positions.

HEIGHTS OF SEBASTOPOL
Field guns and army encampments on the plain of Sebastopol (below). Some experts believe that, had the Allied forces attacked as soon as they arrived at Sebastopol, the Russians would have been quickly defeated. As it was, the Allies opted to establish supply bases and settle in for a siege, allowing the Russians time to prepare their defences.

ENTENTE CORDIALE
English and French soldiers enjoy a drink together (right) during the siege of Sebastopol in 1855. In general, the French army was far better equipped and supplied for the war, and they did what they could to help out their British comrades.

WRAPPED UP
Captain Brown of the 4th Light Dragoons (seated, left) with his servant in winter dress, 1856. By the end of the war, British troops were much better equipped, but officers were criticised from the outset for living in comfort while their soldiers suffered.

SISTERS IN CARE
After Florence Nightingale (left) and her nursing team arrived at Scutari in Constantinople, the care of the wounded men did improve. The reduction in death rates, though, was largely due to the removal of a blocked cesspit that lay beneath the hospital. Nightingale's team was one of several that went out to the war. A nursing team was led by Mary Stanley, who staffed the hospitals on the Crimea itself, and others were run by the Sisters of Charity.

Another heroine of the Crimea was Mary Seacole (bottom left), a Jamaican who had learned nursing skills based on traditional medicine from her mother. In January 1855 she made her way to Balaklava at her own expense and set up the 'British Hotel', a NAAFI-style store providing food, warmth and comfort for the tired, the hungry, and sick and wounded soldiers. 'Mother Seacole' even nursed the wounded on the battlefield – Turks and Russians, as well as British.

RELIGION AND POLITICS

YOUNG GLADSTONE
William Gladstone in 1852, the year he succeeded Disraeli as Chancellor of the Exchequer in the coalition government headed by Lord Aberdeen. Gladstone had intended to reduce income tax, but instead had to raise it to pay for the Crimean War.

In 1850 Lord John Russell's government had to deal with the sudden resurgence of an old problem. Papal territories and the rights of the Roman Catholic Church had been reduced across Europe, and Pope Pius IX was making efforts to regain some of the lost power and influence. On 29 September, 1850, he issued a Papal Bull entitled *Universalis Ecclesiae* to launch the restoration, after more than 250 years, of the Catholic hierarchy of England and Wales. Pius created a Cardinal-Archbishop of Westminster and 13 other diocese, including Liverpool. Coincidentally, there was a surge of pro-Catholic sentiment among members of the intellectual Oxford Movement, who sought to align the Anglican Church more closely with Catholicism.

The Queen, raised a Lutheran, was generally tolerant of other religious views, but complained when the new Cardinal proposed that prayers for Her Majesty should follow prayers for the Pope. Britain as a whole was still strongly anti-Catholic and reacted with hostility to the papal bull. Prime Minister Russell called the move 'papal aggression'. In the Parliamentary session of 1851 he introduced an Ecclesiastical Titles Bill, which made it a criminal offence for Roman Catholic bishops to adopt territorial titles such as Archbishop of Westminster. (The Bill was repealed by Gladstone in 1871, but not before Catholics in public office had been persuaded that the British government would never be their friend. The Queen got it right in her journal, a biographer thought, when she wished that the Pope had done privately and quietly what he had done 'so offensively' in public.)

Religion in the House
The liberalisation of attitudes to religion had begun in the 1830s. Benjamin Disraeli, whose parents were Jewish but had converted to the Anglican faith, was appointed Chancellor of the Exchequer in Lord Derby's government in 1852, the first Jewish person to achieve high office in government. In 1858, after years of struggle, the banker Lionel de Rothschild became the first Jewish MP to sit in the House of Commons.

Rothschild had first been elected in 1847 as one of four MPs for the City of London, but he could not take his seat because MPs had to swear the Christian oath. In 1848 the Commons passed Lord John Russell's Jewish Disabilities Bill to allow Jewish MPs to use a different oath, but the Lords rejected it three times. A decade later, in 1858, the Lords agreed to allow each House to decide which oaths to recognise. The reform finally opened the way for Rothschild to enter the Commons: on 26 July he took the oath on the Old Testament, using the Hebrew word for 'God'.

In 1852, Benjamin Disraeli became the first Jewish person to achieve high office in government as Chancellor under Lord Derby.

Extending the vote – the Chartist movement

The people's right to vote was the burning question of the 1850s. The 1832 Reform Act had made major changes to Britain's franchise system, reallocating seats to the growing new towns and granting the vote to most owners and occupiers of property or land valued at £10 a year or more. But many men – and all women – were still without the vote. The Chartists were a working-class movement who had campaigned since the 1830s to change the parliamentary system. They demanded a vote for all men over the age of 21, electoral districts of equal size, voting by secret ballot, abolition of the rule that MPs must own property and for MPs to be paid a salary. The last two points would make it possible for a working-class man to win a seat in Parliament. There were other glaring inequities in the system, too – many small parliamentary seats were still the property of aristocratic landowners and were never contested.

By the 1850s, the Chartist movement had lost much of its impetus, but their ideas had taken root. Lord John Russell introduced a bill to extend the vote in 1852, and another in 1854. Then in 1859 Disraeli, who was leader of the House of Commons in the Earl of Derby's second government, proposing sweeping reforms including disfranchising 70 small boroughs and transferring their seats; extending the '£10 rateable value' rule; and giving the vote to lodgers who paid at least £20 a year in rent, to university graduates, to government pensioners and to men with savings deposits of at least £60. The radical John Bright dubbed Disraeli's proposals the 'Fancy Reform Bill'. The Liberals, realising that some townsmen would lose their vote, condemned the bill, bringing down Derby's government. But the way had been paved for more franchise reforms when the Earl of Derby bounced back to lead a third Tory administration in the 1860s.

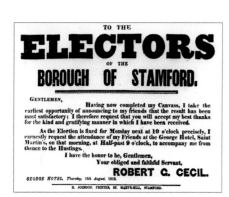

THE HUSTINGS
A public notice from Robert Cecil (above), MP for Stamford in Lincolnshire, during the election of 1855 which brought Palmerston to power as prime minister. Cecil was returned unopposed in the election of 1859. Below: A prospective parliamentary candidate (the man directly above the lamppost) makes a speech from a balcony at a rally in London, in about 1858.

RICH
AND
POOR

At the apex of Victorian society sat the landed aristocracy; at the bottom of the pyramid lay the struggling mass of rural and urban poor. In between, a many-layered 'middle class' strove to better themselves, and in surprisingly many cases, as social mobility increased, they succeeded. Whoever they were, their station in life was instantly recognisable by their dress.

LIFE OF LABOUR A country woman poses for William Grundy's camera in 1857. To the left is a wash dolly for stirring clothes in a wash tub.

The 1851 census revealed that the population of Britain (which then included Ireland) stood at 27.4 million, an increase of more than 50 per cent since 1801, when the first census was taken. Density averaged about 44 people per square mile, but people were not evenly spread across the land: half the population was crowded into 70 cities of 20,000 or more residents. About 35 per cent of the population was under 14 and only 5 per cent was over 65, compared with 17 per cent under 14 and 16 per cent over 65 today.

The Britain of 1851 was a nation of large families. A small minority lived, like the royal family, on country estates and in city palaces. Millions of the middle classes lived in comfortable town houses or in the suburbs then being built on city outskirts. Only about 10,000 men and women had an income of more than £300 a year (about £23,500 today) and thereby earned enough to be assessed for income tax. The poor areas of cities were overwhelmed by the rural-to-urban drift of poor country people, most of whom ended up crowded into terrible city slums.

THE RICH

The aristocracy were Britain's great landowners. They made their money from rents and farming and, from the late 1700s, from mines, quarries, canals and railways on their estates. As late as 1873 around 200 aristocratic families totalling less than 0.5 per cent of the population – a few with incomes as large as £50,000 a year (about £4 million today) – controlled 43 per cent of the land in England. Rich bankers, merchants and industrialists also bought up land: the aristocracy taken together with these lesser and new landowners (the 'gentry') – about 12,000 families in all – owned 70 per cent of Great Britain.

From the ranks of the aristocracy and gentry came ministers for government, administrators for the Empire, and, through the purchase of commissions, officers for the army. They invested their wealth in industry and in ports, shipping and transport. And they supported traditional country pursuits such as horse-racing, riding to hounds, hare-coursing, hunting and fishing.

> From the ranks of the aristocracy and gentry came ministers for government, administrators for the Empire, and, through the purchase of commissions, officers for the army.

Aristocratic patronage

The rich were great patrons of architecture, spending vast sums on rebuilding country seats and palatial town houses. Many rich Victorian industrialists built elaborate mansions, like William and George Gibbs who made their fortune importing guano – sea-bird droppings much in demand as fertiliser. William purchased Tyntesfield in Somerset in 1843 and had the house rebuilt over a number of years in Gothic Revival style. In 1847–50 Charles Barry, architect of the new Houses of Parliament, designed Bridgewater House in London in

THE GOOD LIFE
An imposing village house enjoys a prominent position near the church in this photograph by William Grundy in 1857. The two boys in the foreground hold a book and bat, emblems of their privileged education. The engraving (left) shows Bridgewater House, the town residence of Lord Ellesmere, overlooking Green Park in London. It was designed by Charles Barry, architect of the new Houses of Parliament.

extravagant Italianate style for the Earl of Ellesmere. Other grand folk were renting white stuccoed houses in and around London's Belgrave Square, built by master-builder Thomas Cubitt for the Duke of Westminster. They immediately became London's most fashionable address – Belgravia.

Some aristocrats were keen scientists and inventors. William Parsons, 3rd Earl of Rosse, was President of the Royal Society from 1848–54 with a particular interest in astronomy. He built a 72-inch telescope, then the largest in the world, through which he was the first to observe spiral galaxies and a far-distant gas cloud, which he named the Crab Nebula. New scientific institutions that came into being at this time with aristocratic support included the Royal Meteorological Society, founded in 1850, and the Royal Photographic Society, founded in 1853 under the patronage of the Prince Consort.

The upper classes were fond of the theatre. The play of the decade was *Box and Cox* by Berkshire playwright John Maddison Morton, a farce about two lodgers who shared rooms, one occupying them by day and the other by night. It was first produced at the Royal Lyceum Theatre, London, in 1847, and was such a hit it continued to be performed throughout the 1850s.

In 1851 Jules Perrot, the celebrated French Director of Ballet at Her Majesty's Theatre in London's Haymarket, left the company to dance at St Petersburg. Under his direction the English ballet had improved immeasurably and was now emulating the artistic standards of the great Paris Opéra or the technically superior Royal Danish Ballet. The Opera House in Covent Garden closed in March 1856 after a disastrous fire. It reopened in May 1858 with a performance of *Les Huguenots* by the German composer Giacomo Mayerbeer.

Art collectors

Many people of influence in the mid-Victorian era acquired impressive art collections and supported contemporary artists. J. M.W. Turner, who died in 1851, spent a productive decade of his life painting in a studio at Petworth provided by the 3rd Earl of Egremont. James Leathart, a company director in the northeast, was much taken by the paintings of the Pre-Raphaelites, the avant-garde artists of the day. The Pre-Raphaelite Brotherhood had been created in 1848 by John Everett Millais, Dante Gabriel Rossetti and William Holman Hunt. Their paintings were controversial at the time, rejecting classicism in favour of medievalism and emotional expression. The first exhibition of Pre-Raphaelite paintings took place in

STAR GAZING
Amateur astronomers pose for the camera in 1857 (right). Astronomy was a popular hobby among the aristocracy, and some took it very seriously indeed. William Parsons, the 3rd Earl of Rosse, had this gigantic telescope built in the grounds of his home, Birr Castle, in Ireland.

1850, when they also won praise from the critic, John Ruskin, but generally they failed to set the art world alight. Ruskin's own influential study of architecture, *The Stones of Venice*, was published in 1853.

History and landscape were the important genres of 19th-century painting, and both remained popular into and well beyond the 1850s. Frederic Leighton's first major work, *Cimabue's Celebrated Madonna is carried in Procession through the Streets of Florence* (1853–55) was an instant hit when exhibited at the Royal Academy – Queen Victoria bought it. She also bought the unusual *Ramsgate Sands* (1854), the first large-scale crowd painting by William Powell Frith, who followed it with *Derby Day* in 1858. Frith's talent for reflecting mid-Victorian life back to the mid-Victorians themselves made him immensely popular with his public.

The painting of the decade might be said to be *Monarch of the Glen*, a portrait in oils of a magnificent Scottish stag by Edwin Landseer. Landseer's paintings of animals quickly became well-known, as the growing middle class displayed copies of them on their parlour walls – the artist's brother made excellent engravings from the originals.

> The painting of the decade might be said to be Edwin Landseer's *Monarch of the Glen*, a portrait of a magnificent Scottish stag.

VICTORIAN PASSIONS
Professor John Obadiah Westwood (left), an entomologist and palaeographer, making notes on a particularly magnificent specimen of dragonfly in 1857. Westwood gained a reputation for his fine illustrations of insects, and was president of the Entomological Society in London.

ARTISTS AND WRITERS
Some of the major artistic and literary figures of the 1850s (left to right, and top to bottom):
1. The painter William Powell Frith (1819–1909).
2. Pre-Raphaelite painter, poet and translator Dante Gabriel Rossetti (1828–82), photographed by Lewis Carroll.
3. The painter Sir Edwin Henry Landseer (1802–73). Renowned for his paintings of animals, Landseer also modelled the bronze lions in Trafalgar Square, London.
4. The historian and essayist Thomas Carlyle (1795–1881).
5. Pre-Raphaelite painter Sir John Everett Millais (1829–96).
6. Author, artist, critic and social reformer John Ruskin (1819–1900).
7. Alfred, Lord Tennyson (1809–92), English Poet Laureate from 1850 to his death.
8. The poet Elizabeth Barrett Browning (1806–61), wife of Robert Browning.
9. The romantic Pre-Raphaelite painter William Holman Hunt (1827–1910).

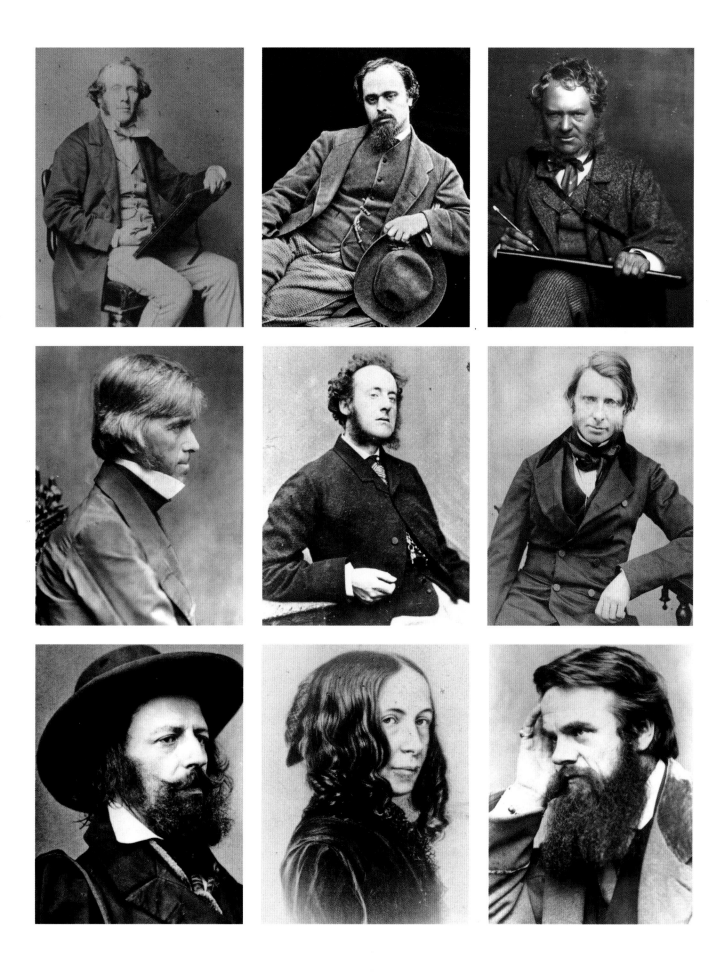

THE WORKERS

Although the idea of a prosperous, hardworking 'middle class' and a poorer, harder-working, downtrodden 'working class' seems quintessentially Victorian, it is hard to define social class by looking at any particular factor, such as income or occupation. Historians point to the clergy of the Anglican Church, who ranged from the generously remunerated Eton and Cambridge-educated John Bird Sumner, Archbishop of Canterbury 1848–62, to parish curates (below vicars in rank), who earned less than many working men. 'Those were the days,' wrote George Eliot in *The Sad Fortunes of the Reverend Amos Barton* (*Scenes of Clerical Life*, 1858), 'when a man could hold three small livings, starve a curate a-piece on two of them, and live badly himself on the third.'

Doctors, too, ranged from rich, titled London surgeons to poor, unqualified village practitioners. Many people worked in small, traditional industries, using techniques untouched by mechanisation. The 1851 census listed 112,000 blacksmiths and 37,000 millers, as well as bakers, carters, wheelwrights, shoemakers, nailmakers, glovers and tailors. Where these workers, along with lawyers, apothecaries and shopkeepers, fitted in the hierarchy is not easy to say.

Civil servants and clerks

The Civil Service was unequivocally upper middle class. In the 1850s it employed fewer than 20,000 people, mainly public school and Oxbridge-educated. As in most areas of commercial life, recruitment was by patronage, not qualifications. But change was in the air. In 1853 a government report called for reform. The service, it claimed, was attracting 'the unambitious and the indolent or incapable'. A competitive examination, vetting of candidates, a probationary period and promotion by merit were recommended. In 1855 a Civil Service Commission was appointed to push the recommendations through; it would take them years.

The Victorians had no difficulty distinguishing lower middle from middle from upper middle class.

The sons of families who could afford it were educated and trained for a suitable career from as young as 13 years – in the law or medicine, for example, or as a clerk in a financial establishment. The term 'clerk' referred to office workers of all types, and this was an expanding sector – the 1851 census listed 44,000. As well as working for the Civil Service they staffed banking, insurance, accountants' and other offices. Civil Service clerks started on annual salaries as low as £10 (about £800 today) if they joined as teenagers, but could work up to £80–£150 (£6000–£12,000) before promotion. Clerks in the Bank of England could earn up to a £250 salary (about £20,000).

But there were also clerks like Bob Cratchett, Scrooge's poor, generous-hearted assistant in Charles Dickens' *A Christmas Carol*. He would certainly have worked a longer day than the six and a half hours (or less) worked by Bank or Civil Service clerks, and earned a salary towards the bottom of the middle-class income scale – less than £100 a year (about £8000 today). It was scarcely enough to support a single man, let alone raise a large family.

CREATURE COMFORTS
A typical middle class drawing room in Norris Green, Liverpool, in the 1850s. The furnishings and decoration reflect the family's status and income. The ornaments and draperies gave such rooms a characteristically cluttered look, which transformed into cosiness in the evenings, when the curtains were drawn and a bright fire lit. This family possesses an unusually fine collection of books.

Building boom

As the towns expanded, the middle classes moved away from the unhealthy commercial and industrial districts out to the more salubrious suburbs, now accessible by tram, railway or omnibus. The 1850s saw a speculative building boom in the cities. In Manchester, Victoria Park was an architect-designed residential area of elegant villas south of the city centre that had been built in the 1840s. Enclosing walls, toll gates and a private police force were planned. The suffragist Emmeline Pankhurst grew up there, and among its residents was the German pianist Sir Edmund Hallé, a refugee from the 1848 revolutions in Europe, who founded the Hallé orchestra in 1858. Another was Henry Enfield Roscoe, Professor of Chemistry at Owen's College (later to become the University of Manchester), who built the first practical chemistry laboratory and in 1858 produced what may have been the first flashlight photograph. Nether Edge in Sheffield was begun in 1836 by George Wostenholm, a local cutler, who bought land to build an estate of socially impressive villas in tree-lined streets modelled on Boston, Massachusetts, for middle-class, self-made businessmen like himself.

Unlike modern social historians, the Victorians had no difficulty in distinguishing lower middle from middle from upper middle class. In London, the upper strata lived in Georgian houses in the centre of town, such as the garden

No. 2. WATER CLOSET FOR ONE PERSON.

Fig. 4.

LATEST MOD-CON

Bathrooms were a rarity in houses in the 1850s, but water closets were becoming a popular fixture in the middle-class family home. This example was exhibited at the Great Exhibition in 1851, after which toilets of varying degrees of sophistication appeared on the market, some using dry soil and some flushed with water.

THE FINAL TOUCH

An impeccably dressed and groomed trio in the late 1850s. One women kneels to make a final adjustment to her companion's skirt. Only second-hand clothes could be bought 'off the peg', but from the 1850s it was possible to buy 'unmade dresses' with the bodice – the trickiest part to sew – already made up and the skirt cut out. As the railways improved distribution, paper patterns were printed in magazines to make dressmaking easier. Gentlemen's clothes could be bought ready-made.

squares of five-storey terraced houses in and around Bloomsbury. The streets were paved, planted with trees and lit after dark. The 'middle middle' lived further out – in Camberwell, Clapham, Denmark Hill. Builders such as Thomas Cubitt, who had built housing in Camden Town and Stoke Newington before his Belgravia masterpieces, laid out suburbs in areas served by railway, tram or omnibus. Mobility was essential in an era of rapid change and most people rented.

The brick and stuccoed middle-class terraces of the 1840s and 1850s were built with private stables in mews at the back and modern conveniences, such as a water supply to the kitchen. Bathrooms rarely featured; people bathed in a tin bath in front of the fire in their bedroom, the water being carried up by a maid. Some houses were built with water closets – a must-have addition to the family home after 1851. At the Great Exhibition that year, 827,280 visitors used the flush toilets installed by Brighton plumber George Jennings. He charged one penny, hence the phrase 'to spend a penny', which made them expensive by today's standards – 1d in 1851 is about 34 pence today. Jennings made himself a profit of £1790 (about £145,000). In 1852, with the support of Henry Cole, the Great Exhibition's organiser, the first public 'Gents' were opened on Fleet Street in London, followed by a 'Ladies' in the Strand.

Home as a haven

The Victorian middle-class house was an intensely private domestic refuge from the commercial world outside. Visitors were invited no further than the front parlour. Victorian women were expected to marry and be supportive wives and fulfilled mothers. There were few alternatives. In the late 1700s less well-off middle-class women had occupations as diverse as jailers, plumbers, butchers and tailors, but by the 1840s they were overwhelmingly concentrated in just four occupations: lady companion, governess, seamstress and milliner. These were considered the only suitable occupations for a respectable woman. The 1851 census recorded 25,000 governesses. After the Crimean War, nursing was added to the list.

Lower middle-class wives and mothers were constantly busy. Contemporary accounts show that they looked after their children, shared the housework with their maids, decorated the home, made soft furnishings, upholstered, cooked, preserved, brewed beer and made wine, laundered, grew herbs and vegetables, and made the family's clothes and linen. Mrs Beeton's instructive monthly supplements on aspects of household management, which appeared in *The Englishwoman's Domestic Magazine* from 1859, were much referred to.

Reading matter

Upper middle-class women, who could depend on maids and nursemaids to do the housework, had leisure time for visiting, shopping and reading. The 1850s saw a boom in fiction, even though books were expensive to buy. Many novelists, notably Dickens and Thackeray, were first published in instalments in magazines. Thackeray's *Pendennis*, Anthony Trollope's *Barchester Towers* and Charles Read's *Peg Woffington* were all popular during the decade, as were several novels by women – *Amos Barton* by George Eliot, *Cranford* and *Ruth* by Mrs Gaskell, and *Villette* by Charlotte Brontë.

The story of Elizabeth Barratt Browning's love affair and marriage, told in *Sonnets from the Portuguese* in 1850, struck a chord with many women. Alfred, Lord Tennyson, whom the Queen appointed Poet Laureate in 1850 on the death of William Wordsworth, captured Victorian melancholia to perfection. His *Charge of the Light Brigade*, which he said he wrote minutes after reading about the incident in *The Times*, expressed the nation's sense of awe and sorrow. It was distributed to the troops in the Crimea as a pamphlet.

But the novel of the decade – indeed, the bestseller of the 19th century – was written by an American. *Uncle Tom's Cabin*, Harriet Beecher Stowe's account of slavery, was outsold only by the Bible. Fifteen hundred copies circulated in Britain in the 1850s. The novel was in tune with the anti-slavery feelings in

continued on page 133

TRADITIONAL WOMEN
Three Welsh matrons taking tea and cake in 1858. The tall hats worn over bonnets, betgwen (an open-fronted dress), apron and shawl were a composite 'national costume' adopted by Welsh women at a time when Welsh culture was under threat from many directions. The influence of Nonconformist religions, especially Methodism, was stifling Welsh folk culture. Depopulation struck the rural centre and northwest of Wales as workers flocked to the industrial valleys of the Anglicised and urbanised Southeast. Welsh children were discouraged from speaking Welsh, following a parliamentary report which claimed that the language was a drawback to the Welsh people, for which the introduction of English was the only antidote. The fight to preserve the Welsh language and culture began to pay off in the mid 19th century, and the first National Eisteddfod was held in 1861.

HYGIENE AND HEALTH

Crucial new discoveries were made about the causes and spread of diseases in the 1850s, but cures and prevention lagged behind. In 1852 John Snow identified water from a polluted pump as the cause of a cholera outbreak, but until proper city sewers were built the problem did not go away. Parliament took a big step towards bringing the scurge of smallpox under control: in 1853 inoculation with Edward Jenner's cowpox virus was made compulsory and free for children under four months old.

FARADAY GIVING HIS CARD TO FATHER THAMES;

KEEPING CLEAN
Without running water supplies, washing clothes was hard, time-consuming work (left). In cities the lack of clean water was an added problem. A national commission, set up in 1844, encouraged the building of affordable bathhouses. By the 1850s some cities, such as Wolverhampton and Newcastle-upon-Tyne, had set up public baths and washhouses with facilities that the poor could use.

UNCLEAN AIR
Traditional waste disposal methods were far too small-scale for Britain's rapidly expanding cities. Filth accumulated and was washed into rivers. Through the hot summer of 1858 the stench from the Thames (left) finally concluded the long-running debate about how to deal with London's overflowing sewers and cesspits. Joseph Bazalgette's radical and hugely expensive plan for constructing new brick sewers beneath the streets was finally given the go-ahead. Work began in 1859.

Infectious diseases were generally believed to arise from 'miasmas' – poisons in the air from evil-smelling sewers, cesspits and rubbish. While some scientists now questioned this theory, it nonetheless inspired some effective treatments. The biggest killer of the 1850s was tuberculosis, or consumption, and the view took hold that removing patients from miasmas could cure the disease. By the end of the decade, sanitariums were being set up to treat patients with fresh air, rest and good food.

FRESH WATER

A domestic servant cleaning fish at a water pump in a scene from William Grundy's 'English Views' in 1857. People depended on pumps and wells for water, and as city populations and industry grew, this became a huge problem. Supplies were often insufficient for the burgeoning populations, and water became dangerously polluted.

A London surgeon, John Snow, was the first to prove the link between polluted water and cholera. Early symptoms of stomach pain and nausea led him to suspect that cholera patients must have eaten or drunk something that made them ill. He became convinced that water infected by poisons – perhaps by 'germs', as some scientists were theorising – was causing the disease. By mapping the houses where deaths occurred, he narrowed down the suspect cause to one communal pump. His research was also later recognised as a groundbreaking example of the science of epidemiology.

Another leading light in the fight against water-borne disease was Edwin Chadwick, who in 1842 had published a report on 'The Sanitary Conditions of the Labouring Populations'. The government of Lord John Russell took up the cause and in 1848 made Chadwick commissioner of a Central Board of Health, with powers to order improvements in water supplies. By the 1850s, his work was having an effect. The Anglezarke Reservoir was built to bring clean drinking water to Liverpool, swollen by more than 1 million refugees from the Irish potato famine. By 1853 Bristol's 'Line of Works', a system of aqueducts and tunnels, was supplying water from the Mendips.

SCOTTISH TRAINING

Sir James Young Simpson, the obstetrician who pioneered anaesthetics in childbirth, was Professor of Midwifery at Edinburgh University. Edinburgh and Glasgow were recognised as centres of medical excellence. Joseph Lister, who later pioneered antiseptic surgery, was a professor at Glasgow, and Thomas Addison, who identified appendicitis and anaemia, trained in Edinburgh.

NEW HOSPITAL

More hospitals were desperately needed for the growing cities. Great Ormond Street Hospital for Children (above) was founded in London in 1852 to help the children of the slums. The hospital was the brainchild of gynaecologist Dr Charles West, who formed a committee including Edwin Chadwick, Baroness Burdett-Coutts and Lord Shaftesbury to raise subscriptions to fund it.

THE SIMPLE LIFE
Itinerant knifegrinders at work outside a stone-roofed English cottage (left), photographed by William Grundy in 1857. The inside of the cottage would have looked something like the living room above. An open fire in the range would have heated water – a tap is visible on the left – and an oven on the right. Blackened kettles hang in the chimney.

Britain following abolition in 1833 – feelings that cut across all classes, from Prince Albert, who patronised anti-slavery societies, to miners in the northeast who collected for charities to help runaway slaves. In 1859 Samuel Smiles, who had been editor of the *Leeds Times*, published *Self-Help*, the first in a series of bestselling books that effectively catalogued what we today call 'Victorian values'.

Skilled workers

The countryside still supported about half of the population in 1851, many of whom worked in the great country houses – some aristocrats and wealthy industrialists possessed more than one, as well as a town mansion. The running of a house required people with specialised employment skills, such as butler, housekeeper and cook. Outside, the estate would require a manager or steward, gamekeeper, groom, stable hands, coachman and gardeners. These employees considered their status to be well above that of labourers and domestics.

Skilled workers were much in demand as the industrial revolution developed and were highly paid, especially in the building and shipbuilding trades, and in luxury trades such as watch and clockmaking, coach-building, printing and

COUNTRY ESTATES

ESTATE STAFF

Gamekeepers (right) deterred human and animal poachers, such as these herons. The great estates still employed a large staff of servants. The photograph below shows the domestic staff of Erdigg Hall, home of the Yorke family in Wrexham, North Wales, in 1852. Unusually for photographs of the time, their names have been recorded, although we do not know which is which. They were head gardener James Phillips, coachman Edward Humphries, laundry maid Elizabeth Alford, dairy maid Mary Davies, head housemaid Ruth Jones, under gardener William Price, footman William Stephenson, head nurse Eliza Rogers, cook and housekeeper Mrs Webster, butler Thomas Murray, lady's maid Elizabeth Hale, under nurse Sarah Evans, carpenter Thomas Rogers and hall boy Edward Davies.

bookbinding. Workers could make substantial earnings – £1 10s a week or more (upwards of £6000 a year today). By the 1850s there were more skilled jobs than ever before. Engineering had divided into a range of specialised industries. Draughtsmen, turners and skilled mechanics could earn more than £3 a week and formed an 'aristocracy of workers'. Boys from less well-off families were sent away from home at an early age to serve apprenticeships in anything from tailoring or printing to the new engineering industries, their fathers paying for them to be bound for five years.

Outworking kept the trickle of poor people from the country to the towns from turning into a flood in the mid-1800s – thousands of farm cottagers in the midlands and the north produced yarn and cloth for a living, or to supplement an income from farm work. Pillow lace-making and glove-making were cottage industries, and in the southeastern counties girls made money by straw-plaiting – making straw strips to be sewn together into bonnets.

Leather-tanning and shoemaking employed many men. Everywhere, in town and country, milliners, dressmakers and tailors were in demand. The conditions in the 'honourable' trades – that is, in workshops under the control of the ancient tailors' and other guilds – were far better than those in the cheaper, or mass-market workshops, which were called 'dishonourable' and 'sweated' trades.

The working class

Working-class men in the mid-Victorian era laboured on the railways and in other industries, as stone quarrymen, miners of coal, lead, copper and tin, carters, cab and busmen, railway porters and seamen. The 1851 census listed some women in all men's occupations. There were 910 women iron miners, 592 women blacksmiths and 590 women railway workers, plus 28 women in shipbuilding and 19 female clerks. In all categories, women were usually paid considerably less than men.

In 1851, 10 per cent of the work force and 40 per cent of women worked in domestic service. Many were in service from as young as ten. In the houses of the rich, the working hours for staff were long, the pay poor and there was little time off, but at least the work was regular and there were perks: adequate food, a bed at night, free clothes and accommodation, and sometimes even a house or small pension in old age. Employing servants was one of the features that distinguished the upper middle classes from the lower,

WHEN WORK IS DONE
The 1830 Beer House Act allowed any ratepayer to brew and sell beer on purchase of a licence costing two guineas (£2 2s). So Victorians set up beer houses in their front parlours, selling beer they brewed themselves. Following abolition of the tax on glass in 1845, brewers began to use glass bottles instead of selling beer in stoneware jars, which changed national preferences from muddy black porters to clear amber light ales.

The aim of the beer house licence was in part to reduce the sales of gin, which was literally killing off the workforce. Beer was also safer to drink than most water. Beer houses became places for working men to rest and socialise – like these men playing dominoes – or read a borrowed newspaper and discuss the issues of the day.

so it was *de rigueur* for a household that considered itself 'respectable' to have at least one servant. There were hundreds of thousands of the lowest-ranking 'maid of all work'.

There were vast differences in standards of worker's housing. In Ireland, after the terrible potato famines of the 1840s, the comfortable farmhouses with well-equipped kitchens made a stark contrast to the single-storey tenants' cottages built of rough stone and rubble – many of them abandoned due to deaths, evictions and mass emigration. Some landowners built villages for their tenants on their estates. The Wingfields of Powerscourt, Co. Wicklow, built the spacious village of Enniskerry between 1815 and 1850.

A Quaker family, the Malcolmsons, founded a model industrial community around their cotton mill at Portlaw, Co. Waterford, in Ireland, with attractive worker's housing. Construction, begun in 1825, was complete by 1860. It became the model for Bessbrook, a planned village built in 1845 around the linen mill owned by the Richardson family, also Quakers. In England, many mill and mine-owners built housing for workers following the example of Robert Owens' model industrial village at New Lanark, Scotland.

THE POOR

At the other end of the scale were the hovels in which many rural workers barely subsisted. In 19th-century England, many agricultural labourers were hired for a year at a time. Local historians in northern England have unearthed descriptions of the dilapidated, single-room 'cabins' provided for these hired workers. They often had leaking roofs and lacked any fixtures, even window frames and fireplaces. A newly arrived family would first have to make the place weather-proof and habitable. Farm labourers generally kept a pig or a cow, which shared the family accommodation.

Poor urban workers lived in inner-city housing areas, close to the factories and workshops. The working-class areas of Lambeth, Chelsea and Brentford in London were beside the polluted Thames and flooded annually. The poorer working class could not afford the transport to the cleaner suburbs, and so had to live near their places of work. In places, cooperative societies acted like building societies, enabling members to buy new 'two up, two down' terraced housing, so some working class people did succeed in becoming owner-occupiers.

The slums

The perpetual drift of rural families to the towns and cities to find work led to city populations outstripping available housing. Liverpool's population was 82,000 in 1801; swelled by Irish peasants trying to escape the famines of the 1840s, it had risen to 376,000 by 1851. Unemployed agricultural labourers and former cottage spinners and weavers looking for work swelled Glasgow's population from 77,000 in 1801 to 329,000 in 1851. In the same period, Manchester's population grew ten-fold from 30,000 to 303,000, while that of Leeds trebled from 53,000 to 172,000.

In northern cities, unscrupulous landlords and builders threw up street after street of poorly constructed back-to-back housing – two terraces of houses each with one entrance, backing on to a common wall – to rent to the masses. Several families would share a house, or even a room. There were minimal shared washing and privy facilities in the back yard. Privies emptied into cesspits, which often overflowed. Old, run-down city-centre housing was rented to poor migrants. In 1844, the German social

continued on page 141

OLD GLASGOW
Close No 65 off the High Street, Glasgow, from a record published in 1860. The population of Scotland's industrial cities, especially Glasgow, rose steadily as the rural population fell. This drift of people from country to town led to overcrowding and turned streets like this one into slums.

EXODUS

Along with manufactured goods and the idea of free trade, the Victorians exported people. In the century from 1815 to 1914, more than 22 million economic migrants left Britain and Ireland – more than 8 million of them bound for the United States. The peak years for this mass migration were the early 1850s. Emigration relieved unemployment and destitution at home, it stimulated international trade and spread British cultural influence worldwide.

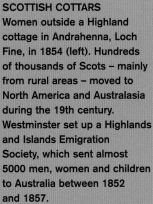

SCOTTISH COTTARS
Women outside a Highland cottage in Andrahenna, Loch Fine, in 1854 (left). Hundreds of thousands of Scots – mainly from rural areas – moved to North America and Australasia during the 19th century. Westminster set up a Highlands and Islands Emigration Society, which sent almost 5000 men, women and children to Australia between 1852 and 1857.

THE IRISH EMIGRANT
Irish-born actor John Drew dressed for a role in 1850 as 'The Irish Emigrant' (above left). Between 1846 and 1851, 5000 'famine ships' carried Ireland's starving poor to America – to New York and Boston, or to Halifax and Quebec in Canada, which was cheaper than to New York. A Celtic cross at Grosse-Ile, Quebec, marks the grave of some of those who did not get the chance to make a new life.

NEW METROPOLIS
Ships moored in New York harbour, as seen from Trinity Church, looking towards New Jersey. Built in 1846, Trinity Church remained the tallest structure in Manhattan until the turn of the 20th century. By 1850 more than a quarter of New York's population was Irish. With 300 or more emigrants arriving on its quays every day, New York became the world's busiest port.

FAME AND FORTUNE

A few emigrants made their mark in their new country. In 1851 Andew Carnegie, son of a Scottish weaver who went to the USA in 1848, started work as a telegraph messenger for the Ohio Telegraph Company. By 1857, now a superintendent on the Pennsylvania Railroad, he was making investments in Pullman sleeping cars. He was rich by the mid 1860s. In 1873 he met Henry Bessemer, and took the new steel-making method back to America. It would make him the richest man in the world. He gave away much of his fortune, some of it to build libraries back in Britain.

ECONOMIC MIGRANTS

People of diverse backgrounds emigrated, from the younger sons of the aristocracy whose older brothers inherited the family land and money, to Cornish miners, whose knowledge of steam-engine technology and its application in deep-shaft mining made them in demand in the silver mines of South and Central America. More than 250,000 Cornish may have emigrated in the 19th century. Many went to California after the 1849 gold rush, to tap deep lodes, then spread through Nevada and Arizona, or crossed to Australia after gold was discovered there in 1851.

Other emigrants were more interested in farming than getting rich quick through gold, and land was on offer in America. Wagon trains pulled by sturdy oxen, like the one below, took European settlers and their few possessions to new homes in the west. Before the building of the railroads, these were the only transport to venture across the continent.

reformer Friedrich Engels described the resulting slums in *The Conditions of the Working Class in England*: 'The streets are generally unpaved, rough, dirty, filled with vegetable and animal refuse, without sewers or gutters, but supplied with foul, stagnant pools instead…'. The governments of the 1850s had no housing policies to deal with the population explosion and cities developed piecemeal. Slum areas were cleared to build roads, railways and new buildings, but there were no re-housing schemes for the thousands made homeless when their meagre dwellings were torn down. Victoria Street in London was built in 1850 through notorious slums from Victoria Station to the Great Exhibition. The displaced residents simply migrated to other slums.

'The houses are occupied from cellar to garret, filthy within and without, and their appearance is such that no human being could possibly wish to live in them.'

Friedrich Engels, describing English slums in 1844

Addressing the housing problem

Victorians from Prince Albert downwards applied their minds to the problem. Outside the 1851 Crystal Palace stood a prototype of a 'Model Dwelling House' designed by Henry Roberts, architect to the Society for Improving the Condition of the Labouring Classes, and paid for by Prince Albert, the Society's president. The house was a culmination of Roberts' pioneering work on philanthropic dwellings. Some built in London were copied all over the world, giving Britain a reputation – perhaps misplaced – for having the best workers' housing in Europe. The dwelling was a four-apartment module, which could be extended upwards and sideways to create an apartment block. The construction was fire-proofed and insulated, and each flat had toilet facilities and roomy accommodation.

The social reformer Anthony Ashley Cooper, 7th Earl of Shaftesbury, supported Acts of Parliament in 1851 intended to empower local authorities to inspect, regulate and establish new lodging houses for the labouring classes. Although these Acts were not immediately effective, charities such as the Metropolitan Association for Improving the Dwellings of the Industrial Classes sprang up and built hundreds of tenements in the capital. Elsewhere, municipal authorities imposed building regulations and sanitary controls, so that areas of adequate housing, with sculleries, privies and coal houses, were built for artisans and employed workers. In Sunderland, for example, many one and two-storey workers' cottages with back yards were built to a regulation minimum size after the introduction of building regulations in 1852.

MODEL DWELLING
The 'Model Dwelling House' that was designed by Henry Roberts, and paid for by Prince Albert, as working class family accommodation. It was erected in the grounds of Hyde Park Barracks for the 1851 Great Exhibition. The prototype was later dismantled and now stands in Kennington Park, London. In 1852, Roberts built an estate in Windsor based on his model dwelling.

Relief for the poor

The Victorians believed that economic and social problems would right themselves without government interference, so they were baffled by the poverty that persisted despite the nation's growing prosperity. They saw work opportunities galore, and concluded that anyone who did not work must be idle.

There was poor relief: since the 1500s, each parish had been responsible for its poor, paid for by raising local rates. But the numbers applying for relief were growing and the rates were an increasing burden, especially in the cities. A Commission appointed in 1832 to look into the problem had decided that the system must be tightened up. 'Outdoor relief' (payments to people in their homes) was to cease except in exceptional cases. People who could not find work ('the able-bodied poor'), or refused to work ('the idle poor'), could receive food and accommodation in workhouses, which were to be built by groups of adjoining parishes. The workhouses would be run by paid officials, who were to make them more uncomfortable and miserable than life outside.

The poor law worked in a way – the numbers of 'poor' reduced by almost 25 per cent. But many workers were not paid a living wage and others were hit by unemployment during trade downturns, so where 'outdoor relief' was stopped, families were thrown on to poor relief. The workhouse regime was harsh and humiliating, and to be avoided if at all possible. Husbands and wives were separated and inmates were forced to do prison work, such as stone-breaking and 'picking oakum' – the futile unravelling of lengths of old rope – in return for food and accommodation. And the system could not cope with large-scale disaster. During the potato famine in Ireland, starving peasants in their thousands hammered on the doors of workhouses too full to take them in.

Charitable giving

Donations by wealthy philanthropists and the public went some way to bridging the gap between the needs of the poor and the provision made for them. Almost all churchgoers and religious organisations, as well as ancient guilds and professional organisations, ran charities. Ordinary people actively supported hundreds of charities, from almshouses to the Young Women's Christian Association, founded in 1855 to offer accommodation and education to working girls. Angela Burdett-Coutts, heiress to the Coutts banking fortune, was a lifelong donor. She also financed model housing in London, the Westminster Female Refuge for 'penitent prostitutes' and a brigade of shoe-black boys. She provided fishing boats and schools to the Irish, and founded the Bishopric of British Columbia. Middle-class Victorians supported the Children's and Invalids Dinner Table and Soup Kitchen, and the Home for Consumptive Females, as well as charities to educate and help prisoners.

LIGHT RELIEF

Life was not all gloom. Country folk had always had time for sports at slack times of year. Rat-catching by trained terriers and cock-fighting were popular. Instead of horses, country men – and women – set whippets racing and coursing.

From the 1850s workers were increasingly given free Saturday afternoons and trains and trams could take them off to the seaside. Brighton, Scarborough and Southport were a few of the many resorts that opened to weekend visitors, some of whom began to bathe in the sea. Resorts such as Weymouth grew up as health resorts, recommended for people who needed fresh sea air.

Music hall emerged in London during the 1850s. It evolved out of the music pubs of the 1830s, which staged comedy, singing, dancing and theatre in their saloon bars. The Middlesex Music Hall on Drury Lane, Covent Garden, opened in 1851, The Canterbury in Lambeth opened in 1852 and Wilton's Music Hall in the West End in 1856.

Some new sports emerged in the 1850s that women could play as well as men. One was croquet, which had a long history in France and reached England in 1852 via Ireland. It caught on quickly because it was an ideal game for Victorian society: it was played out in the fresh air, yet was slow and dignified enough to be played in long skirts, even crinolines. Another was battledore and shuttlecock, an ancient game which became popular in the 1850s for similar reasons to croquet. By the end of the decade it had evolved into badminton.

EGYPTIAN HALL, PICCADILLY.

LONDON, LITHOGRAPHED & PRINTED BY C.J. CULLIFORD, 22, SOUTHAMPTON S. STRAND.

MOBILE MUSICIAN
Street musicians like this cellist, photographed in the 1850s, were a common sight in ports and other cities, along with singers, dancers, jugglers and acrobats, who were always ready to entertain the crowds and passers-by. Some of the musicians would have belonged to orchestras and bands that entertained the middle and upper classes at more formal concerts, sometimes doubling as street performers to augment their earnings.

STAR OF THE CIRCUS
Zoebida Luti (left), the 'Circassian Beauty' of the 1850s, at the Egyptian Hall, Piccadilly. The Egyptian Hall began life as a museum housing the private natural history collection of William Bullock, a former goldsmith and member of the Linnaean Society. In 1812 he had commissioned the architect Peter Frederick Robinson to design a building based on an Egyptian temple. He opened it as the 'London Museum', but later sold the collection and instead hosted exhibitions on exotic subjects such as the tomb of Pharaoh Seti I, ancient Mexico, and Lapplanders with sleds and reindeer. Eventually, Bullock sold the building and it became a venue for panoramas, art exhibitions and productions such as PT Barnum's famous travelling circus, starring Zoebida, who was billed as 'the only lady magician in the world'.

Gentlemen played billiards, which became widespread in the mid 19th century. Billiard balls were made of ivory, but the first step towards a synthetic ball was patented in 1856 by an English chemist, Alexander Parkes, who developed Parkesine, a celluloid, from guncotton and camphor. This would be used to make billiard balls by the end of the next decade.

Boating regattas were held on many rivers in summer, but a thrilling new sailing race was established in 1851 when a 101-foot schooner yacht from the USA, *The America*, raced 15 yachts of the Royal Yacht Squadron around the Isle of Wight. The Americans won by 20 minutes, creating the America's Cup.

MONEY
AND
COMMERCE

By the 1850s, the Bank of England had become the world's first central bank and was the government's most powerful asset in efforts to stabilise the financial system and prevent bankrupties. It was at the heart of a varied and growing network of City, provincial and savings banks that powered commercial expansion.

CITY SHOPPING Regent Street, one of the best shopping streets in 1850s London, busy with horse-drawn cabs and pedestrians.

GOLD RUSH

I n January 1851 a man called Edward Hargraves, who had emigrated from England to Australia in 1832, returned to Sydney from the booming California goldfields, enriched not with gold but with the knowledge of how to find it. Within a few weeks Hargraves had identified gold deposits in and around Bathurst, New South Wales, and a new gold rush was on. Before the year had ended miners by the thousand were prospecting in New South Wales and further afield in Victoria. Before the decade was out a second American gold rush was sparked off by finds in Colorado, where the deposits turned out to be so widespread that new finds were still being made into the 1890s.

By the mid-1850s, the world was awash with gold, much of which was minted into coins. A British Royal Commission on gold and silver, looking back on events from the viewpoint of 1888, calculated that the 1850s gold rushes had increased the world's stocks of gold from £144 million in 1851 to £376 million in 1861.

The Bank of England had long had a policy of holding large quantities of gold. Its banknotes had been made legal tender in 1833, and the bank kept enough in reserve to ensure that they could be exchanged for gold at a fixed price. This prudent practice had given Bank of England notes an international reputation for

GOLD DIGGERS
Edward Hargraves inspired a stampede of prospectors to New South Wales, Australia, when he announced the discovery of gold there in 1851. Six months later, further deposits were discovered in Victoria. These goldminers were photographed in Ballarat, Victoria, in about 1855.

stability when gold had been in short supply and too expensive for most other countries to follow. By 1856 the price of gold had fallen, making it feasible for other countries to adopt a gold standard.

Gold oiled the wheels of international commerce. Dealers in England's regional stock exchanges were now extending their operations to the mining industries, railways and insurance. Confident that speculative investment bubbles – like the still-notorious South Sea Bubble crash of 1719-20 – could not happen in the 1850s, English and Scottish banks invested heavily in the emerging American market. In 1857 that confidence was severely jolted by the first international monetary crisis.

An international crisis

In September 1857, the SS *Central America*, carrying 3 tons of gold, much of it coinage and bullion for New York banks, ran into a hurricane and sank. The news flashed across America on the new electric telegraph. Just a month before, an American life insurance company had failed due to embezzlement. Already unnerved, the Americans now panicked. On 1 October, more than 400 banks in New York and New England suspended payments to their customers, many of whom were queuing outside the barricaded doors. New York stock prices plummeted – fortunes were lost.

British banks could not escape the fallout. As in America, there were runs on banks and one, in Glasgow, failed. In the crisis the Bank of England emerged as a force for stability, accepting notes issued by banks besieged by panicking customers and exchanging them for its own, trusted, currency. But to be able to act so generously as the nation's 'lender of last resort', the Bank was forced to suspend its own rules on gold reserves and print notes without the equivalent gold to back them. Luckily, the crisis was short-lived.

POSITION OF RESPONSIBILITY
Sir John Herschel (1792–1871), pioneer photographer and astronomer, was also Master of the Mint at the Bank of England from 1850–55. He is shown here holding a florin coin in 1852.

A NEW KIND OF BANK

By the 1850s the Bank of England had become the world's first central bank. It was the nation's main banknote issuer and a bulwark against bank failures. It had eleven branches in major provincial cities, which had been founded after a banking crisis in 1825–26; initial hostility had dissolved into cooperation in the face of their calming influence at such times. In an emergency, the Bank had found, it could raise interest rates on its loans to agency banks and brokers, indirectly tightening credit across the country. Yet it was still a private bank, making a profit through commerce and issuing notes.

In 1850 most banks remained private institutions, but Coutts, Hoare's and other West End of London banks, who catered for a clientele of landowning aristocrats and wealthy gentry, were being superseded by a new wave of commercial banks in the City of London. These dealt with trade, handling bills of exchange (payments for international commerce) and loans to stockbrokers. City banks also played a role as London agents for a new breed of country bank that had mushroomed in the provinces to give farmers and industrialists credit to fuel their businesses. Many of these provincial banks were started up by tax-collectors, drapers, solicitors and brewers – people who accumulated money in payments in the course of their business and could loan it out as a sideline. Fosters Bank in Cambridge, for example, had been founded by a family of millers and grain merchants; Lloyds of Birmingham by Quaker iron founders; and Smith, Payne & Smiths of Nottingham by hosiers.

Banks outside London could still issue their own banknotes, but few kept enough gold to cover the value of the notes printed. During sharp downturns many had insufficient gold to meet panic cash withdrawals by customers. Without enough gold to back them, their banknotes became scrap paper. The problem was that legislation, dating back to before the South Sea Bubble crisis, encouraged English banks to stay small. By law, they had to be private partnerships of no more than six people, with each partner personally liable for losses – and many banks still operated on this basis.

Limiting liability

After 1826 banks with more than six partnership members were permitted outside a 65-mile radius of London. These operated on the Scottish 'joint stock' model, by which many investors could contribute different amounts of capital to set up a bank. Profits were divided in proportion to amount invested and the number of shares owned, so the risk of bankruptcy in a crisis was lower. By 1857 there were 98 joint-stock banks operating in the provinces and in the confident climate of the decade, new legislation permitted liability for partners' debt in joint

continued on page 154

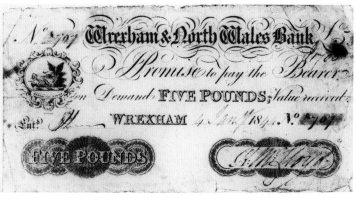

PRIVATE NOTE
A £5 note issued by the Wrexham & North Wales Bank in 1844. Up until then, private and provincial banks were allowed to print and issue their own money. That year, the right was restricted by the Bank Charter Act, which prohibited new banks from issuing their own currency, and limited the amount that existing banks in England and Wales could issue. It would still be some decades before printing notes became the exclusive right of the Bank of England.

EVOLVING FINANCIAL SERVICES
A group of men outside the head office of Backhouse's Bank of Darlington in the City of London (right). The bank had been founded in 1744 by James Backhouse, a Quaker flax dresser and linen manufacturer. It later merged with Gurney's Bank of Norwich – founded in 1770 by Quaker landowners, the family of prison reformer Elizabeth Fry – and Barclays of London.

The Bank of England occupied a gracious neo-classical building begun by the architect Robert Taylor and completed after his death, in 1788, by John Soane. The engraving (left) shows the Bank as it appeared in 1855. In 1853 another renowned financial institution, the Stock Exchange, moved into a new building in the City of London. The stock market had evolved into a regulated exchange with formal membership, codified regulations and daily trading, with branches in Manchester, Liverpool, Birmingham and Leeds. Its motto remained *Dictum meum pactum* – 'My word is my bond'.

FREE TRADE

Until the 1850s, Britain's merchants and shipbuilders were shielded from competition by the Navigation Acts. Under these 'barbaric old laws', as the economist Adam Smith had described them, only British ships could carry foreign goods into ports in Britain and its colonies. Cushioned by this protectionism, Britain's merchants failed to see that with China opening up and the East India Company's monopolies gone, the valuable Eastern trade in silks, porcelain and tea was open to all, including the Americans, who built the fastest ships in the world – the tea clippers.

British shipbuilders, restricted by an old tonnage law that taxed ships according to length and breadth, built merchant ships that were short, deep and slow. The cargoes were also burdened by excise duty. Ever since the Civil War, monarchs and parliaments had used excise duty to finance wars, and by 1800 the British were paying tax on practically everything.

By Queen Victoria's reign, the ideas that Adam Smith had voiced in 1776 – that goods should be produced and priced to benefit the consumer, that lifting trade barriers would make poor workers better off – had taken root in the principle of *laissez faire* and found a champion in Richard Cobden (right). In 1846 the Corn Laws and their tariffs on imported cereals were repealed. These had been introduced in 1815 to prevent cheap cereals cutting landowners' profits. Their repeal seemed to symbolise the freeing up of trade.

In 1849, now convinced that free trade would increase prosperity, Lord Russell's government repealed the Navigation Acts. For the first time in 200 years foreign ships could unload at British ports. In December 1850 the first US tea clipper, *The Oriental*, sailed into West India Dock carrying a load of tea. She had raced from Hong Kong in just 97 days – Britain's Blackwall frigates took almost a year to make the trip. By

1850 tea from China had displaced coffee among Britain's discerning and better-off classes, and they preferred their tea leaves fresh and uncontaminated by long storage in a ship's hold.

Britain's shipbuilders were keen to copy the streamlined American ship, but the tonnage law tax remained until 1859. Only then did it become profitable to build tea clippers in Britain, helped by the abolition of duty on imported timber the same year. The duty on some foodstuffs, such as sugar, was also abolished, but it remained on tea, coffee, wines and spirits – luxuries that accounted for more than 90 per cent of customs revenue.

By the end of the decade, Britain's exports had doubled. British commerce was swept up on a tide of growth as the government dismantled trade barriers, and all but the most profitable of excise duties, to create the freest trade regime of any industrial country, before or since.

CHAMPION OF FREE TRADE

Richard Cobden (left, 1804–65) founded the Anti-Corn Law League in 1838 to campaign for the repeal of tariffs on cereal imports that kept bread prices artificially high. Cobden rose from a poor background – he had attended one of the Yorkshire schools on which Dickens based 'Dotheboys Hall' in *Nicholas Nickelby* – to become owner of a calico-printing mill and was inspired by Adam Smith's *Wealth of Nations*. He based the Anti-Corn-Law League in Manchester and from there launched a campaign that saw him delivering lectures to packed halls, forging links with trade unions and lobbying MPs and the press. As MP for Stockport from 1841, he spoke movingly in Parliament on improving working people's lives by freeing trade. This cartoon (right) of August 1852 ridicules politicians' reactions to his philosophy and their unwillingness to jump into the free trade waters.

In 1847 Cobden set about exporting the idea of free trade itself. He travelled the Continent initiating negotiations for trade treaties between Britain and other countries. If we depend on each other for food and other essentials, he argued, war will eventually wither away.

THE AGE OF SAIL

A coastal schooner sails up the Thames past Greenwich in about 1860 (left). Many square topsail schooners like this one were built on Prince Edward Island, Canada, during the early 1800s and sold to British merchants. They were light, fast and manoeuvrable, and used for coastal trading. The Americans built a version with raked (sweptback) masts called the Baltimore clipper – and it was from a Baltimore shipyard that the first large, ocean-going clipper sailed forth in 1833.

The White Star Line was one of several shipping companies formed to meet the rush to the Australian gold fields. The White Star directors chartered and eventually purchased this fast American clipper (right), called the *Red Jacket*. The illustration shows the ship negotiating ice off Cape Horn at the tip of South America, *en route* from Australia to Liverpool in 1854. She could make the journey one-way in about 70 days.

stock companies to be limited to the size of their investment. This 'limited liability' inspired the creation of thousands of new companies in the next few years.

Innovative, risky, but above all exciting, banking soared ahead in the 1850s. Thomas Joplin, who had set up the National Provincial Bank of England in 1833, was forging ahead with a scheme to open branches all over England and Wales. By 1860 he had more than a hundred, including, of course, an administrative branch in the City of London. By 1860 so many financial institutions had taken offices in the City, the resident population there began to plummet, while the population in the rest of the country was rising rapidly.

Small savers

The Reverend Henry Duncan was a Victorian man of note. He restored the 8th-century Ruthwell Cross and presented the first scientific paper on fossil footprints to the Royal Society in Edinburgh. He worked to help his parishioners in Ruthwell, near Kirkcudbright, by negotiating cheap bulk grain, providing flax for the local women to spin and employing the men to turn his land into a model farm. But perhaps his greatest achievement was with the village Friendly Society.

Friendly societies and saving schemes were not new, but generally there was an element of charity in how they were run. Duncan, who had once worked in a Liverpool bank, conceived of a self-supporting savings bank run on business principles as a way of helping his parishioners to help themselves. Regular saving would alleviate their poverty by building up interest at a commercial rate. In May 1810 he opened the Ruthwell Savings Bank – sixpence would open an account, and members received 4 per cent interest from the Linen Bank in Dumfries where the money was deposited. The scheme was a success and widely copied. By 1850 hundreds of banks had opened all over Britain under the umbrella of the 'Trustee Savings Banks'. They were immensely successful, accumulating more than £30 million of micro-savings by 1847.

Other innovators aiming to help the poorer classes included the Cooperative Movement, founded in Rochdale, Yorkshire, in 1844. It began by selling food at wholesale prices, but later introduced services such as credit and housing. Edward Akroyd was a worsted manufacturer in Halifax, who set up allotments and

THE COOPERATIVE MOVEMENT
The Rochdale Pioneers, who founded the first retail Cooperative movement in 1844. One of the problems they set out to tackle was the commonplace adulteration of food. Uniquely for a food retailer, the cooperative shop advertised unadulterated butter, sugar, oatmeal and flour – at fair prices the working class could afford. Later, they began to offer credit and housing services.

pension schemes for his workers. He founded the Yorkshire Penny Bank for them in 1853. From total savings of just £151 in the first year, small savers accumulated £3 million over the next decade in a national network of 'penny banks'. Akroyd built model housing for his workers, then expanded on the idea, launching a scheme with the Halifax Permanent Building Society to help small savers to buy their houses.

Women investors

In 1851, some 40 per cent of women aged between 20 and 40 were single. More than a million were spinsters and some 750,000 were widows. Without a husband, women had no social status, but they did have legal status and could own property. (On marriage, a woman lost all rights of ownership, including of her children, to her husband.) Fathers and husbands commonly left property or legacies in trust for wives and daughters. Single women with property could make money running lodging houses or dame schools – 100,000 women were listed as teachers in the 1851 census – and insurance records show women occupied in a variety of trades.

The accumulated wealth of all these women influenced the economic development of the country. Women tended to invest in safe options, such as Bank of England Consols – bonds issued as part of the national debt at a fixed rate of interest. By 1840, half of the investors in the national debt were women, who held 32.1 per cent of bonds issued, with individual holdings averaging just under £5000. Women figured prominently in the crowds that gathered at the Bank of England on Dividend Days. Women may not have had the vote, but increasing numbers of self-supporting women were an economic force in mid-19th-century Britain.

WOMEN IN A MAN'S WORLD
Lady Angela Georgina Burdett-Coutts (1814–1906), with her companion Mrs Brown (standing). In 1837, she inherited a fortune which made her the richest woman in England. She spent much of it on charities and other good causes. In 1871, Queen Victoria made her a baroness in recognition of her philanthropic work.

MARKETS AND MILKMEN

FRESH AND LOCAL

Food on sale in 1850s Britain was seasonal and local, as in this thriving Christmas market in 1856 (right). Grain prices were low in the early years of the decade and bread came fresh from the bakehouse. Butchers bought meat 'on the hoof' from livestock markets or from local farmers, who drove their animals directly to the butchers to be slaughtered and dressed for sale in shops, market stalls or street barrows. Animals were as common a sight in the towns as in the country. Rabbits, hares and poultry, dead and alive, were sold on the streets by hawkers, along with grouse, pheasant and partridge during the shooting season.

Country people shopped in small local fairs and markets, where farmers sold their produce and 'cheapjacks' (or 'johns') set up shop from their horses and carts selling pots and pans, cutlery and crockery, tools, bridles and grooming implements for horses. The annual local horse or pig fair – like the Irish Pig Fair at Abbeyleix in Queen's County (below) – was a highlight of the year.

DAILY MILK DELIVERY

In towns, hundreds of milk shops and dairies had stalls at the back where cows were kept for milking. Milk was delivered to customers' doors by milkmen, or women, bearing yokes and pails, like the man pictured on the right. The woman is churning milk into butter.

In country areas, where distances were greater, milk might be delivered by donkey. This boy in Wales (below) is returning home after his round. Ass's milk was popular in Victorian times for its health-giving properties. It is closer to human milk than the milk of any other animal – sweet and low in fat – and was given to suckling infants, ailing children and invalids. It does not keep well, so the milch ass was often milked at the customer's door for instant delivery. There was a belief that children thrived on ass's milk, and it is now known that donkeys do not carry tuberculosis, which was the number one killer disease of Victorian Britain.

INDEX

PICTURE ACKNOWLEDGEMENTS

Abbreviations: t = top; m = middle; b = bottom; r = right; c = centre; l = left

All images in this book are courtesy of Getty Images, including the following which have additional attributions:
37r, 55t, 57bc, 59bl, 59bc, 65mc, 91, 97bl, 123ml, 123mc and 155 – Mansell/Time & Life Pictures
153l – George Eastman House

LOOKING BACK AT BRITAIN
VICTORIANS COME OF AGE – 1850s
was published by The Reader's Digest Association Ltd,
London, in association with Getty Images and
Endeavour London Ltd.

The Reader's Digest Association Ltd
11 Westferry Circus
Canary Wharf
London E14 4HE
www.readersdigest.co.uk

First edition copyright © 2007

Reprinted with amendments 2008

Endeavour London Ltd
21–31 Woodfield Road
London W9 2BA
info@endeavourlondon.com

Written by
Helen Varley

For Endeavour
Publisher: Charles Merullo
Designer: Tea Aganovic
Picture editor: Jennifer Jeffrey

For Reader's Digest
Project editor: Christine Noble
Art editor: Conorde Clarke
Indexer: Marie Lorimer
Pre-press account manager: Dean Russell
Product production manager: Claudette Bramble
Production controller: Katherine Bunn

Reader's Digest General Books
Editorial director: Julian Browne
Art director: Anne-Marie Bulat

Colour origination by Colour Systems Ltd, London
Printed and bound in China

We are committed both to the quality of our
products and the service we provide to our
customers. We value your comments, so please do
contact us on 08705 113366 or via our website at
www.readersdigest.co.uk

If you have any comments or suggestions about
the content of our books, email us at
gbeditorial@readersdigest.co.uk

CONCEPT CODE: UK 0154/L/S
BOOK CODE: 638-003 UP0000-2
ISBN: 978 0 276 44251 3
ORACLE CODE: 356900003H.00.24